To Tell the Truth

To Tell the Truth

A Compilation of Inspirations about the Birth of Songs from the Heart, Soul, and Mind of a Storyteller

V. Michael McKay

GIA Publications, Inc.
Chicago

G-5748

GIA Publications, Inc.
7404 S. Mason Ave., Chicago, IL 60638
www.giamusic.com
ISBN: 1-57999-132-7
Book layout and design: Robert Sacha

Printed in the United States of America

Dedication

To my grandfather, Wilmer Schaff Washington
"Papa"
Whose constant love, abiding faith and
living by example inspired the song in me.
And
To my mother, Helen I. Jones
"Miss Jones"
Who always told me to tell the stories of the songs.

Table of Contents

Part II: The Proclaimed Truth

Part III: The Mediated Truth

I Sing It...I Proclaim It

The truth will stand forever. That's why I crave it...I sing it...I proclaim it...I live it! When I begin to envision ministering the Good News of Jesus Christ to the people, I know it must first happen within me. We live in a time where we see people standing for what they think is the truth—living for it, even dying for it. So when I appear before the anticipatory audience, I press to first have that relationship with Christ, then to cultivate it through prayer, meditation, and the study of God's Word.

For this reason, the songs of V. Michael McKay have long appealed to me, such as: "Before I Tell Them," "The Battle Is the Lord's," "Through the Storm," and "Thank You." They are embedded in the Word of God. The Word is their very foundation. Therefore, they will possess longevity, because God said His Word would stand forever. I know when I sing the songs that are in *To Tell the Truth,* they will serve as food for the people of the world rather than just a tickle in their ears. Listeners shall be able to respond to them day after day, letting the message of the songs plunge even deeper into the core of who they are and where they are. Only the Word of God can divide soul and spirit.

I realize that Michael uses a mode of operation in ministering where he actually *asks* God for the next step rather than allowing his flesh to formulate an idea, then asking God to approve it. When you are in the flow of the will of God, He alone *anoints* (a word that is used habitually) you for the assignment. And the assignment always involves telling the Truth!

When we tell the Truth, meaning the Truth of God, we live with the assurance that it will not return void. Souls will be saved, needs will be met, and deliverance will come! When we plant seeds of Truth, we shall reap a harvest of physical and spiritual blessings! God promised it in His Word!

Michael, my fellow workman in the ministry, I'm so glad you decided to write this book in order to tell people the means of God working with you to create these noteworthy melodies that speak to the soul. I'm elated that "Since the last time I saw you," you are still walking in the glad journey of daring To Tell the Truth!

—Yolanda Adams

Preface

I stood up and walked to the witness stand. My knees were quivering, and my heart pounded inside of me like the beating of a drum that rose louder than my thoughts! Could I do it? Was the task too much for me? I was conjuring up the memories, provoking those feelings that lay dormant for so long, and prodding my mind to the point of frenzy. As I viewed the courtroom, the judge sat, waiting to hear what I had to say and knowing all the time what had happened. You see, He is Omniscient.

The bailiff walked up and asked me to place my left hand on the Bible, raise my right hand, and swear to tell the truth, the whole truth, and nothing but the truth, so help me God! As I declared this, I looked into the face of the judge. I couldn't help but notice the bailiff's badge. It said, "The Comforter." The concept of it was all too painful for me! How could I re-tell my story without incriminating myself and at the same time help someone else? I understood my reason for being there! I knew I was already guilty, but I wanted to get it straight! Somebody could learn from this account. Even though nameless, I had to take the chance!

I took a few deep breaths and began. My soul rose higher and higher as I told of each event. At some point, even for me, it began to heal. The ghosts of the past no longer had the detestable hold on me that they once had. Those in the courtroom began to lean on the edge of their seats, wanting to hear more and more of my testimony. They did not want to miss one word. As time went on, they too knew I was guilty. Even the jury knew it, but they had to sit there and listen. I finally reached the close and it was time for the final statement from my counselor, the Prince of Peace! He spoke for me, and as I listened, I intermittently smiled, cried, and shouted. They warned me of being removed from the courtroom because of my excitement. The beauty of it all was that my counselor represented me so effectively! He spoke on my behalf like someone with my best interest in mind!

Now relive my testimony as I tell the truth, the whole truth, and nothing but the truth, so help me God! I hope that like me, when it's time for you to appear on the witness stand, the jury finds you guilty, too. Guilty of being in love with Jesus Christ! For you see, the penalty is not death. It is eternal life!

Acknowledgments

First and foremost, I would like to thank God, for giving me the gift of song. I am forever grateful to my grandparents, Papa and Mama, who helped me to grow in the Lord, to trust in the preacher, and to give heed to the words he or she speaks. I am very appreciative to Ms. Jones, my mother, who is the darling of my heart, for dedicating her life to the calling of her children. I acknowledge my sister Carolyn Cyrus, my spiritual advisor, who helped recall the stories and write them. Thanks to my sister Kathy McKay-Smith, whose practicality and humor grounded me in difficult times. I thank Aunt Christine Cockrell, who planted seeds of music in me early in life and continues to provide inspiration. And to my cousin, Camille Rosenthal, thank you for graciously and humbly taking the time to help edit this book.

I thank Pastor Charles Jackson, who showed me how to approach my gift and to work with the preacher in synchronizing word and song. Pastor Ralph Douglas West further encouraged me to perfect my gift, to form a partnership in ministry between word and song, and gave me the freedom to exercise it. Special gratitude to Reverend Joe Samuel Ratliff, who challenged me to think through each process and justify and defend them. Thanks to the many other preachers whose lives and messages gave inspiration to these songs.

I owe a debt of gratitude to the Redeemed Family, who interprets the songs, and whose lives are reflected in many of these songs. My sincerest gratitude to Stepheny Scott, who dared to document many of these truths and translate them into musical expressions. Thanks to my friend K. Edward Copeland, who helped me to distinguish between the power and the presence versus the presentation and the performance. To Carol Gonzales, my friend, colleague, and sister in Christ; I love you.

Dr. Margaret Douroux, my mentor, who modeled the "gospel song," challenged me to document these songs, and trusted me to share her songs.

To my excellent and helpful associates Anthony Turner and Pamela Bell for their enduring patience as they helped in writing, typing, editing, and preparing the manuscript for publication; and to Tony Hourston for allowing me to impose on his time while wrapping up this text.

And last, but definitely not least, thanks to all or any who have sung these truths!

—V. Michael McKay
Houston, Texas

Part I
The Lived Truth

Introduction: Fleshing Out the Word

By Carolyn C. Cyrus

Have you heard the saying, "Talk is cheap, but it takes money to buy land!"? Talking is one thing, and doing is another. I've often pondered over the scripture that says, "The Word became flesh and dwelled among us." Do we actually let soak within our hearts what that meant to Jesus? Talk is one thing, and doing is another. Jesus had to be the fulfillment of all that the Word said He was. When He was on earth, or, "dwelled among us," He healed the sick...Jehovah-Rapha. He fed thousands...Jehova-Shalom. He raised the dead...El-Elyon. He was "The Good Shepherd"...Jehovah-Rohi. He was Emmanuel, "God with us"...Jehovah-Shammah. Jesus was doing the Father said He would do all the time!

Now what about us? Are we "fleshing out" the Word of God by doing what God said we would do? These are the issues we face everyday...the lived Word. Faith. Trusting God. Forgiveness. Giving. Helping others when we don't feel like it. Loving the unlovable. Touching those who need to be touched by humanity so they can know God in a greater way. The lived Truth is now fleshed out in us so they can know God in a greater way. What an awesome testimony!

This section, "The Lived Truth," is to me the most vulnerable, most inspiring, most exposed section of this book. It reminds me of Jesus' bare back when it was exposed to the Romans. What happened to His back, i.e. the whipping and tearing apart of His skin, is what heals us today. "And with His stripes, we are healed," (Isaiah 53:5). I'm gaining a better understanding everyday. As I look in the mirror and see myself, see my hair turning gray, I know that the lived Word is a hard but inspiring and rewarding walk for us to take. Sometimes is it difficult to "walk the walk" after we've "talked the talk." As we present our bodies as living sacrifices to God, we answer the hardest part of the Word. I believe that Jesus had to flesh out, and when He did, He became the ultimate sacrifice. "So whosoever believes in Him shall not perish, but have everlasting life!" (John 3:16). As we travel in the realm of the abundant life today, I'm encouraging you, brothers and sisters, to flesh out "the lived Truth" with exceedingly great joy!

Songs of the Lived Truth

These songs are the consummation of my living with an attitude of openness to the work and Word of God. Songs of the Lived Word are melodies of perpetual testimony, telling of our never-ending quest to live for God in a world that does not know Him. The inspiration for these songs comes at the most unexpected times. When the temptation arises for me to function independently, and when I am inclined to go my own way, God interrupts with a message in song.

Most of these songs are birthed out of painful episodes in my life. It is at that time God manifests Himself as truly sovereign, omnipotent, omniscient, and most of all, omnipresent. He speaks to me in unmistakable ways, telling me in audible words what to tell His people to encourage them, to exhort them, to deliver them or sometimes just to tell of His unconditional love.

These words transform into songs—songs born out of passionate experiences, songs written by design rather than by chance.

Another Chance

We arrived at Greater New Bethel Baptist Church in Los Angeles, California about 3:00pm. It was Wednesday, October 24, 2001. Moments later, Dr. Margaret Pleasant Douroux, my friend and mentor, sat at the electric piano and began to melodically and passionately play this hymn style tune. It was time to begin devotion for the early evening rehearsal a her annual Heritage Music Foundation Conference. Her musical interpretation of the test baffled me to the extent of wondering, when asked who wrote the song, whether she had actually penned it. The worshippers then began to repeatedly sing the chorus, then the two verses, as the power of the Holy Spirit invaded the sanctuary. The timely text resounded in the room with much clarity and transparency. God's presence was obvious to each of us. The song was then reborn within my spirit.

In retrospect, the Brookhollow Baptist Church choir and myself gathered at the Bingle Street address for our weekly choir rehearsal. The day and date I don't recall. The year was about 1996. I sat at the grand piano and began to play a song, of which I don't remember, as devotion began. A member offered prayer to God. And again, God showed up. Worshippers began to testify of His goodness, His grace, and His mercies. I continued to play as several members voiced their sentiments about God our Father and thanksgiving to Him. The final testimony erupted from Toxie, a choir member who happened to be my cousin. She publicly thanked God for her family, for their prayerful support of her and her daughter, Mikelle. Her heartfelt expressions significantly impacted the souls of the saints evidenced by the tear filled eyes and joyful cries. I continued to play, complementing the mood of true worship. As Toxie concluded her testimony to the gratitude of God, seemingly unable to find appropriate or deserving words, she bellowed out with power, *I thank God for giving me another chance just to say...Thank you!* At that very moment, the Holy Spirit created a Holy matrimony between her words and the music I was playing. With fear and trembling, I began to sing the closing words of her testimony. The choir effectively joined me in singing that chorus. Days later, the Holy Spirit completed the work that He had begun in us and spoke to words to the verses.

In these two unique instances, the people of God entered the sanctuary with outburst of spontaneous praise, whether expressed musically like Margaret, or verbally like Toxie, subsequently experiencing God, the continuous Creator. I, like Toxie and Margaret, will forever thank *God for another chance.* Please join me as we together express our thanks to the Father for each opportunity to Say to Him:

Another Chance

There are those who missed this opportunity
Lord, I realize it could have been me
So in exchange for all that You've done for me
I'll take this opportunity to say...Thank You

Health and strength...friends and family
Lord, to name a few...You've been good to me
for the debt you paid at Calvary
I'll take this opportunity to say...Thank You

Thank You, Lord...for giving me another chance
Another chance...another chance
Thank You, Lord...for giving me another chance
Another chance to say...Thank You

Go in Peace

Blessed be God, even the Father of our Lord Jesus Christ, the Father of mercies, and the God of all comfort; Who comforteth us in all our tribulation, that we may be able to comfort them which are in any trouble, by the comfort wherewith we ourselves are comforted of God....
2 Corinthians 1:3-7

As a musician, I sometimes find it difficult to simply enjoy music without evaluation. In an attempt to explore other genres of music, relax and be entertained, I attended a concert. It was that concert, that experience, which prompted something within me that I could not shake. Though entertained, I was deeply affected by what I felt; who I saw.

Regretfully, I never met her. I saw her only once while performing at Houston's Jones Hall. She was one of two artists performing that evening. I sat down front, capturing her beauty close-up. She deeply mesmerized me with her presence. Her eyes told a story that I unfortunately was unable to read. Her stature, her posture, her stance was almost intimidating. Her beauty was, without question, in the eyes of all who beheld her. Her voice was powerful...strong, certainly complimenting her beauty. Her voice rang out with much clarity, haunting me even days thereafter. I do remember how focused she appeared to be throughout her entire performance. "A true artist,"...I must admit.

Days, weeks, months, even years passed, yet I held on to what I felt that night at Jones Hall. She had captured a part of me, but surely she never knew, for we never met, and I was merely one of thousands pleasured with her beauty and talent. Then finally, the startling news broke; she was dead. The cause of death was reported: suicide. A part of me seemingly collapsed at that awful news. Though death is inevitable, I pondered why such beauty would do such a thing. How could she remove herself from this world, prematurely robbing others of an opportunity to experience her beauty and talent? What devastated her to the point of choosing to take her own life? What in life could be so bad?

Then I, the Christian, began to answer my own questions. I further understood the power in the presence of God. I began to minister to myself. There I stood thanking God for the power in His Word. Even when I do not feel His presence, His Word reminds me that He left His peace with me (John 14.27). There I stood thanking God for my life, knowing that without Him in my life, I too would be a candidate for suicide. There I stood remembering the times I too considered options other than the power in His presence and Word. The more I thought, the more I thanked God for keeping me.

How I profoundly ministered to myself. Please allow me now to minister to you, just in case you're considering options other than the peace of God. Though I never personally met the lady in this story, there are others just like her. Maybe I will be introduced to one or some of them through this song; maybe you are that one. I missed the opportunity to witness to her, but thank God, I will not miss that great opportunity to say to you....

Go In Peace

Before you give up the fight
Before you throw the towel in
Before you give over to the enemy
Before deciding you cannot win
Please consider the Word of God
Like a sheep...Listen for the shepherd's voice
You'll hear Him say what he said to me "Go in peace"

Before you give up on life
Before you lose the will to go through
Before you give into life's failures
Before deciding that's best for you
Please consider the Word of God
Like a sheep...Listen for the shepherd's voice
You'll hear Him say what He said to me "Go in peace""

Go in peace...lay that burden down
Go in peace...don't you know you're Heaven bound
Why feel discouraged, defeated all alone
Like a sheep without a shepherd lost, far away from home
You're God's child, He wants to bless you,
With life eternally
He'll say to you what He said to me
"Go in peace "

Shalom, my brother
Shalom, my sister
"Go in peace"

Good News

How beautiful on the mountains are the feet of those who bring good news, who proclaim salvation, who say to Zion, "Your God reigns!"

Isaiah 52:7

I met her while a student at Texas Southern University, Houston, Texas, in 1971. She was Director of Activities at the Student Life Building. Her name, Mrs. Lillian Johnson, became a household word for many of us while pursuing our college degrees. The role she played in our lives was as important, and in some cases, more than any instructor on campus. Though she did not formally teach a class, what we learned from her was a pre-requisite for graduation. Though it was not offered in the school's curriculum, thank God it was available to us. Mrs. Johnson taught Life 101. Her parental presence overwhelmed us to the point of controlling our behavior. Her spiritual countenance challenged us to the point of ultimate respect for ourselves and others. Still her human qualities were so powerful that we found it quite easy to talk with her about any and every subject, from our personal to our private issues. And didn't we have many issues!

Soon after the semester began, I was introduced to Mrs. Johnson while planning an activity on campus. The university was approaching the celebration of its twenty-fifth year in existence. A part of the festivities included the formation of a gospel choir. I was brought to her specifically to help organize the choir. So we did. We began spending quality time together prior to, during, and following rehearsals. This was the beginning of a long, loving relationship. I was then a member and Minister of Music at Pleasant Grove Baptist Church. My spiritual relationship with Mrs. Johnson grew rapidly, later influencing her to even join Pleasant Grove. There she further affected my spiritual growth and development. She eventually became a friend to my family. She and Ms. Jones, my mom, shared frequently, bonding with each other in unique ways. Needless to say, those ladies had a lot in common. I recall feeling the impact of the powerful energy present whenever they got together. I also recall how life's principles were re-enforced as I overheard their conversations. Their life experiences were not only interesting, but were full of wisdom. They both shared a secret. They both loved to play cards. One needed much wisdom and skill in an attempt to challenge them in that regard also.

There's one thing I distinctly remember about Mrs. Johnson. She had great love and respect for God. Her frequent response to situations culminated with..."Oh God, You've gotta help me." When asked why she spoke to God with such authority, she responded, "I've done all that I am supposed to do, so I can hold God accountable to His Word." Such demonstrated faith in the power of God's Word still consoles me in my daily walk. She often prefaced dialogue about God, Jesus Christ, and the Holy Spirit, with two words 'Good News.' There weren't many, if any, conversations shared with Mrs. Johnson without reflections of the 'Good News' of Jesus Christ. Whether discussing an issue concerning me, one of her own children, a student, a church member, the pastor, or even herself, the 'Good News' of Jesus Christ dignified all of her thoughts.

Mrs. Johnson became gravely ill during the latter part of the 1980's. I'll never forget how I felt when I received the news of Mrs. Johnson's illness and finally her death. Though I grieved, I had so many fond memories and precious thoughts of her, grieving became minimal. She left me with so much hope and expectation in the 'Good News' of Jesus Christ...the Word of God!

On the Friday evening preceding her home going service, I shared in worship with a congregation in Fort Worth, Texas. That experience eased and buffered the anticipated pain that I was to experience the next day. Early that following morning, I arrived at the Dallas/Fort Worth Airport and boarded an American Airlines flight in route to Houston. The service for Mrs. Johnson's home going was scheduled for about 11am. To my surprise, the 7am flight I was scheduled to depart on had mechanical problems and was canceled. What should have been an hour flight became four hours of torture. I didn't arrive at Houston's Intercontinental Airport until 12 noon. I frantically departed the plane, hurried downstairs to the nearest exit, flagged down a cab, and headed for Pleasant Grove Baptist Church. I arrived at the church at about 12:30pm, only to view the funeral recession in progress. My heart was further broken with disappointment. I never got the chance to bid farewell to Mrs. Johnson and sing the song I had written about her to the family, the friends, and the congregation. You probably didn't know her, but through this song you'll surely know about her. This text voices her sentiments.

Good News

I bring to you 'Good News'
Of Jesus and His love
I bring to you 'Good News'
Of His precious, cleansing blood
But since for me, He paid the price
I claim but one earthly right
That's to spread the 'Good News' of Jesus
All the days of my life

I bring to you 'Good News'
Of Jesus and His grace
I bring to you 'Good News'
He died that we all might be saved
But since for me, He paid the price
I claim but one earthly right
That's to spread the 'Good News' of Jesus
All the days of my life

'Good News'...Jesus loves you
'Good News'...He loves me too
'Good News'...I'm not my own
'Good News'...to Christ I belong
I may be absent from this body
'Good News'...I'm present with the Lord
Then throughout the ages
I can thank Him for His love

I'm Stronger

We are hard pressed on every side, but not crushed;
perplexed, but not in despair; persecuted,
but not abandoned; struck down, but not destroyed.
For we who are alive are always being given over to death
for Jesus' sake, so that his life may be revealed
in our mortal body.
2 Corinthians 4:8-11

To tell the truth, the simplicity of this story reveals the beauty of life. I am privileged to be a full-time musician. Moreover, I am blessed to be a full-time "thinker." Being a Christian first, then a songwriter, greatly affects the content of my thoughts. They are always driven by "Truth"—the good news of Jesus Christ. When I hear "Truth," I stop immediately to document that "Truth." No matter what I am doing at the time, I use whatever is available to write on. Though I am gifted to write these thoughts, they are not necessarily mine. Dr. Winfred Hope, a pastor, teacher, illustrator and theologian from Athens, Georgia, told the Redeemed Family at a retreat about ten years ago that gifts are not ours. Their Owner will one day return for them with concern as to the manner in which we, the stewards, used these gifts while they were in our care.

When the inspiration came, I was lying in bed clicking the remote control through several television cable channels. It was Tuesday, August 19, 1997. Bishop Carlton Pearson was preaching on TBN. His message was prefaced by words from the guest who had preceded him. He voiced these sentiments, "I'm stronger because of what I've been through." Gaining strength from those words, I immediately turned off the television. I knew to turn the channel from TBN to H-E-A-V-E-N! A voice within me said, "Yes, I'm in agreement." That is just like the omniscient Father. He ushers in the right words to fall on my hearing at the right time. At that very moment, I was encouraged to exhort others by what I heard.

It was then that the Holy Spirit breathed into me a new way to entreat God's people to press on. I went immediately to the piano to begin the work, and the first verse and chorus were born. That same night, I sang this song at the mid-week service at The Church Without Walls. The next night I taught it to the church choir. Oh, how we were blessed!

Still consumed by this "Truth," I wrote the second verse two days later. This time, I locked into the awareness of the importance of being a good steward. Submitting to the Holy Spirit, seizing the revelation of the moment, and allowing the Giver to connect with the gift unfolded new blessings to me. This gift I share with you....

I'm Stronger

I'm stronger because of what I've been through
I'm better, my faith has been renewed
Though resources depleted, I'm not defeated
Though wounded, I'm feeling brand new
My past brings bright hope to my future
For I know what my God can do
I'm stronger because of what I've been through
Praise the Lord, for it's all because of You

Confronted by life's sudden disappointments
I'm propped up on ev'ry leaning side
Though trouble has found me, I've got peace all around me
Knowing God is my preeminent guide
On yesterday, I had my share of failures
On today, I know I will survive
I'm stronger because of what I've been through
Praise the Lord, it's all because of You

I've had so many dark days and lonely nights
You stood in my place when I was too weak to fight
You led me in the way that was best for me and
Kept me from the hand of the enemy
No weapon formed against me shall prosper
With You Lord, I'm more than a conqueror
I'm stronger because o what I've been through
Praise the Lord, it's all because of You

Integrity

I know my God that you test the heart and are pleased with integrity. All these things have I given willingly and with honest intent...O LORD...keep this desire in the hearts of your people forever, and keep their hearts loyal to you.
1 Chronicles 29:17, 18

It was a sunny Wednesday evening in June at the Brookhollow Baptist Church. Pastor Ralph West and I sat in his outer office comparing hymns to sermon texts as we carefully planned for upcoming worship experiences. The plans were going smoothly...we thought. He would identify the profound and prophetic points to Holy Spirit-inspired, Scripture-based, and well-contemplated sermons. We would then search for related hymns.

Suddenly, we were at a standstill! One sermon's subject was "Integrity." Pastor West's preparation was thorough and complete; however, in diligently searching the hymnal for an appropriate song, we found nothing. We probed our memories for songs from the past, but were unsuccessful. The sermon was to be preached the following Sunday. Understanding the importance of waiting on the Lord to speak, we ended the meeting doing just that. I waited and trusted that the Holy Spirit would dictate the hymn in time—And He did.

On Saturday, three days later, a song was born. To tell the truth, it was not just a song, but also a petition, a prayer set to music. I sang it the following Sunday without the aid of written music or words.

"When we first heard the words and the melody of this song, we sought for the perfection that drives this poignant message." (A congregant) Consider this petition:

Integrity

When I come before Your throne
Asking forgiveness for my wrong
I want to be honest with You, Lord
No matter how hard it may be for me to do
I want to open up to You
And be honest with You, Lord
For You already know my heart, my thoughts
My desires, my sentiments
Thy whys for everything I've done
This is my earnest plea—Let me live with integrity

When life's pieces just don't fit
Give me courage to admit
Dear Lord, I need a change
For it's You who holds the range
Of my possibilities and You own my destiny
I want to be honest with You, Lord
For you know what lies ahead
Trials, temptations, failures
But most of all You know my victories
This is my earnest plea—Let me live with integrity

Make me honest in the things I say and do
Make me honest with myself
I want to be honest with others too
Keep me sheltered from pride
For it comes before a fall
I want to hold my head up high
Keep me standing tall
This is my earnest plea—Let me live with integrity

Intercession

And the Lord turned the captivity of Job, when he prayed for his friends; also the Lord gave Job twice as much as he had before. Then came there unto him all his brethren, and all his sisters, and all they that had been of his acquaintance before, and did eat bread with him in his house; and they bemoaned him, and comforted him over all the evil that the Lord had brought upon him; every man also gave him a piece of money, and every one an earring of gold.

Job 42: 10,11

My family and I always worshiped together. My mother and sisters sort of looked to me for direction in selecting a church home. It was an unspoken tradition carried over from our past. Our grandfather, "Papa" was the patriarch of the family and I inherited that position post his death. Then too, my involvement in church ministries affected that role. But then, after thirteen years of service, my tenure at Pleasant Grove Baptist Church was interrupted. I was invited to serve as Minister of Music at Brentwood Baptist, a Southern Baptist church located in the neighborhood where I lived. With Pastor Jackson's blessings, I left Pleasant Grove in August of 1984 and joined the staff at Brentwood. For the first time in my adult life, I moved away from my immediate family to worship.

That time in my life initiated a great deal of personal growth. I was moved out of my comfort zone. The families who had prayed for me, the pastor who had nurtured and sheltered me, the church members who had tolerated my initial periods of trial and error, were nowhere around. I grew up real fast. God loved me enough to plant me in a place to enhance my spiritual growth and development and I took full advantage of that opportunity.

Eleven months had passed. Then one summer evening, Mrs. Susie Jefferson and Mrs. Alberta McElroy, two of the fine Christian women at Pleasant Grove, invited me to be the musical guest for the choir's annual day. I graciously accepted. With a sense of newfound maturity and excitement, I arrived at Pleasant Grove for first choir rehearsal. It was the second Wednesday night in July of 1985. The choir's anniversary was always on the third Sunday in July. There in the choir loft were those wonderful people who I had shared with for thirteen years. Many good memories invaded my mind. After sharing some of them, I began to teach music in preparation for the concert on the following Sunday. That's when the struggle began. To my surprise, I didn't recognize the sound of the choir. It was foreign to me. Their sound lacked joy. It was spiritless. There was no freedom of expression. Even the countenances on the faces of the choir members were different. Their faces were sad and somber. They appeared to be unhappy. I knew them in times past to express themselves in a Godly fashion through sound as well as in their presence. I knew this was true because I had trained them for thirteen years. Together we explored and discovered effective ways to express ourselves in worship. As the night grew older, I thought that things would change for the better, but they didn't. The rehearsal ended. We departed.

The sights and sounds of the people I knew and loved invaded my mind, consumed my thoughts, and interrupted my rest. I knew upon departure from the church on that night God had strategically ordered my steps in that direction for a purpose. I had to intercede for them. It was my responsibility to pray for my family members. I tried to sleep through those thoughts, but couldn't. Finally, I was awakened by an invasion of new thoughts and sounds. It must have been the Holy Spirit. He guided me into the presence of the Father. I began to dialogue with Him. He listened as I talked. Oh, how I poured out to Him! I documented those words that I shared with Him. Again a song was born. Sleep then fell on me and I rested well. Yes! This is a prayer...a prayer offered by all who will read it, and sang by all who will sing it. By the way, God honored my request and answered my prayer. Prior to the concert on the third Sunday in July 1985, Pleasant Grove's choir was full of joy. God re-awakened their hope in Him as a deliverer and restored their joy.

Every now and then I find myself praying through this prayer all over again!

Intercession

Lord, I've come on behalf of my brother
Even though I have needs of my own
But real joy means you first Lord, and then others
I'm not here for myself but for someone else
Once you've meet the needs of my brother
I'll rejoice knowing soon you'll meet mine
I've come on behalf of my brother
Praise You Lord, for You always bless on time

It's not mine to question how you test us
It's just mine to live by Your Word
You send sunshine for some and rain for others
Yet I know You're just and we'll all have both in time
In the midst of my gloom, give to my brother
Everything he needs to make it through
I've come on behalf of my brother
Praise You Lord, for all blessing comes from You

Real joy means placing You first Lord, and then others
I'm not here for myself
I'm interceding for someone else
Heal broken hearts, change doubtful minds
Touch dying souls, make my brother whole
I've come on behalf of my brother
For real joy means placing You first Lord, and then others
I'm not here for myself but for someone else

Lifting Jesus

Just as Moses lifted up the serpent in the wilderness, so the Son of Man must be lifted up, that everyone who believes in him may have eternal life.

John 3:4-5

I spent summers as a child with my grandparents in Alexandria, Louisiana. During my last three years of high school, when my parents separated, I was able to spend a more extended time with my grandparents. They had almost thirty grandchildren, some of whom they reared. We called them Mama and Papa. They made each of us feel special. They had ten children of their own, so they were experienced "raisers." Mama was the world's greatest grandmother; those who did not get the opportunity to know her have my sympathy.

Papa was a Baptist preacher. He pastored in rural towns near Alexandria for over forty years. I spent all day Sundays assisting him, beginning the morning with family prayer meeting. Following breakfast, we positioned ourselves in Papa's car and made our way to Marksville, Glenmora, or Moreauville. We were usually the first to arrive at church, customarily an hour or more before Sunday School started so that Papa could spend time alone in prayer. Oh, how he would preach the good news! My joy was carrying his briefcase from the house to the car, then into the office at the church, sometimes to the pulpit. This procedure would reverse as we left the building to return home.

What I remember most about Papa is that he was the same at home and at church. Nothing seemed to change about him. He was as loving and compassionate at home as he was at church.

Weekdays began with the sound of his voice as the wake-up call. We shared breakfast prepared by Mama. Much love! He kissed me on my forehead with loud smacks as I approached the back door en route to school. He waited for me to return home so we could talk about the cares of my day over dinner. Periodically, we spent Friday nights together in the rural towns where he pastored as he visited and prayed for the sick. Saturday evenings were our time together as he taught me the Sunday School lesson. Much love! There are no other moments to compare to these!

I left Papa after graduating from high school. He deeply encouraged education. He deposited me at Southern University in Baton Rouge, walked me through the registration process, and supported me wholly. After the first year there I joined my mom and sisters in Houston. I continued my education and began a rewarding life in church music ministry. Within ten years, Papa retired from pastoring.

Mama, Papa's soul mate, became ill and left us in 1985. Shortly thereafter, due to failing health, Papa was placed in a nursing home where he spent his final days. Consumed by an image of a strong, healthy, powerful, God-fearing preacher and father figure, I found it difficult to see him. One spring day in 1988, I drove from Houston to Alexandria to visit him. Little did I know that I would never see him alive again.

I entered his room wearing a pair of jeans and a tank top. I greeted him with a big smile, but he did not recognize me. I repeated my name several times, but he had no recollection of who I was. A stab of pain surged through me like a mighty rushing force unlike any I had known before. As we stared desperately at each other I felt time stood still. My smile faded—just when I felt I could no longer restrain the tears, Papa said, "Oh, yes, you're Michael, my grandson, my colleague in the ministry. Look at those arms! I can tell you've been lifting Jesus." My tears subsided, and we had a loving visit.

That was the last time I saw Papa alive. But thanks to Jesus Christ, that is not the last time I will see him. While I await our next visit, he lives within me through all of the wonderful thing he taught me. When I least expect it, another principle taught by Papa is influencing me, or I am sharing one of our experiences with another person. So it was in the case of our final visit.

Sparrow Record Company's owner, Billy Ray Hearn, invited me to Nashville, Tennessee, just after the company had moved from California. He extended to me the opportunity to be the initial and premier writer at their new Nashville writing facility. I accepted his offer. I called my Christian friend and brother, George Stewart, and informed him of my plans to visit Nashville. We carefully planned our time together during my short stay. The visit was powerful. Early morning, while in route to Sparrow's office, George asked me to tell him one of my "Papa" stories. I gladly began to tell him about the last time I had seen Papa alive. Immediately, the spirit of God powerfully overwhelmed the both of us, even while riding in the car.

When we arrive at the office I departed from George, still feeling the presence of the Holy Spirit. Together, the Holy Spirit and I walked into the building on that wonderful morning. I greeted the attendant, was escorted to the writing facility, sat down at the piano, and began to play and sing the words to this song as the Holy Spirit dictated. I don't recall when He, the

Holy Spirit, left me alone on that day, but I do recall how wonderful His presence felt.

Let the words of this song minister to your heart. The essence of the praise is associated with the relationship between God and me, even though it was invoked by the relationship between Papa and me.

Lifting Jesus

I had a talk with someone that I loved
But he did not know who I was
With tears in my eyes
I prayed he'd recognize me
For I, yes, I was his child

Then in a while he looked into my eyes
And let me know that he knew me
The tears left my eyes
And joy filled my heart
For he knew that I was his child

He said, "I can tell you've been lifting Jesus"
No greater words had ever come my way
Lord, let Your Spirit overwhelm me
In such a way that men will say
"Child, you look like...
You've been lifting Jesus"

My Epitaph

Death and Destruction lie open before the Lord -
how much more the hearts of men!
Proverbs 15:11

I have a friend who married about 16 years ago, but her marriage failed. She had a child that her husband accepted no responsibility for, so she was forced to rear the child on her own without moral, spiritual, or financial support from her ex-husband. She was broken and bitter.

She encountered more trial—her home burned; she became emotionally disordered, she had no money. She sought solace by dabbling in the occult, but this hurt her even more deeply, as now she was spiritually bankrupt. To make matters worse, she called me one Friday night to read a tabloid article to me, which alleged that her ex-husband had abused a child.

I asked her if she would like to change places with the mother of that abused child. Of course, she would not. In ministering to her over time, I told her that in spite of our circumstances, situations, and conditions, God writes the last script for all our lives.

This conversation so haunted me that I wrote all night. My Epitaph was born that night. I called her on Saturday morning and sang it for her.

To tell the truth, God has the last word for all of us. Since then, she and I have become better friends.

My Epitaph

He wrote the script and set the stage
By His design each character was named
He was there when my story began
And He alone knows how it will end

He made the world just like a stage
At His command life's curtain is raised
Then you will know how my story began
But He alone knows how it will end

He created my life and placed me on stage
For this reason I'm not afraid
My life, an epistle, God writes with His pen
For He alone knows how it will end

As He writes it...read it
An open book, a testimony...see it
Each day a new episode
My epitaph He writes with pen in hand
For He alone knows how it will end

One Thing I Know

"...One thing I do know. I was blind but now I see."
John 9:25

My grandfather was and still is the greatest influence in my life. "Papa" proved to be a man of integrity, earning my uttermost respect. I don't ever recall doubting anything he ever told me. He planted seeds into my spirit that have brought forth fruitful harvests. He deposited within me an array of holy, helpful hints that will forever be resourceful to me. He shared information with me regarding Christian principals that still influence and sometimes even govern my present behavior.

After graduation from high school, I left my grandparents' home and attended college in Baton Rouge, LA. Within a year, I left Louisiana and moved to Houston, TX. God soon thereafter orchestrated my steps in a new direction and led me to a wonderful ministry led by a powerful preacher man. Little did I know that I would spend the next sixteen years of my life there. Pastor Charles Jackson and the Pleasant Grove Baptist Church family was no doubt my family; my home away from home. Pastor Jackson nurtured me as though I was his own son. There were times I felt smothered—sheltered, as though he was protecting me from something, like Papa had done for years. He definitely was not "Papa," but possessed similar Godly qualities, eventually winning both my heart and affections. His fatherly image coupled with his spirituality invoked a trust in him similar to that trust I had in Papa.

Pastor Jackson has a great salvific testimony. For sixteen years I heard it. For sixteen years I saw signs or symbolism around it. He was saved on the back of a dump truck while working for Houston Lighting & Power Company. In other words, he had a life-changing encounter with Jesus Christ on the back of a dump truck while working for HL&P. Pastor A. Louis Patterson, a theologian in his own right, visited the church during one of Pastor Jackson's anniversaries. Pastor Patterson presented him with a little toy dump truck, which sat on the pulpit podium for years, symbolic of his salvific experience. During my sixteen-year tenure at Pleasant Grove, I heard others tell where they first experienced God. Then layman, now Pastor Ben Roy Lilly celebrated being saved on the sandy banks of the San Jacinto County. Mrs. Provost, a faithful member, took pride in letting us know that she had an encounter with the Lord in a beer tavern with a beer bottle in her hand. Their testimonies weighed heavily upon many of us who heard them, leaving us with the one ultimate question. Where or when were we saved?

Years passed before I consulted anyone concerning the question that had so long haunted me. Maybe I feared having to justify my own salvific posture. Finally, I asked the one person who I knew would be honest with me. He knew of my love, commitment, and dedication to Jesus Christ. He had personally walked me through the Roman road, assuring me that I was saved based on the Word of God. I, along with Carolyn, my sister, finally asked Papa to answer the one question that had plagued us for a long time. How do I explain my salvation providing I don't know or remember the place, time, or circumstance surrounding the experience? Papa, while standing in the kitchen, gazing over the top of his eyeglasses, responded immediately after seemingly deep contemplation. He shared with us experiences from his past. He told us about those who were saved while working in the fields in Louisiana, and how they ran through those fields rejoicing thereafter. To our surprise, he intimated that he, like us, had no initial salvific experience. Papa then pointed us to the little boy in the scriptures who was born blind. When the lad's parents were asked to explain the circumstances surrounding his obvious deliverance, they replied, "He is of age, ask him." The boy, in turn, responded, "I don't know. One thing I know, whereas I was blind, now I see." Papa's brief but profound explanation liberated both of us. I left my grandparents' kitchen with those words on my heart and went directly to the piano in the living room and began to spontaneously compose this song. Together, my sister and I sang this brief yet profound text with heartfelt resolution.

One Thing I Know

One thing I know
One thing I know
I was blind
But now I see
There's no doubt in my mind
I've been born again
There's no doubt in my mind
I've been born again

Born again
Born again
Born again
There's no doubt in my mind
I've been born again
There's no doubt in my mind
I've been born again

Redeemed

He redeemed my soul from going down to the pit,
and I will live to enjoy the light.
Job 33:28

It has been a tradition for my mother's family to celebrate Thanksgiving Day together in a small Louisiana town called Bayou Goula, south of Baton Rouge. We all gather from near and far at one of our relatives' houses to dine sumptuously, update each other about recent happenings, listen to the same stories told annually about childhood experiences, and to respectfully remember those loved ones who are no longer with us. It is always a great time of fun and fellowship filled with love and laughter.

Eventually, pockets of people sharing similar interests are sighted throughout the grounds, sometimes isolating themselves for hours. This was also the case with my Uncle Cullen and me. He is a brilliant theologian, and as usual, we talk about Christian concepts and new discoveries. Uncle Cullen is consistent in one important regard—he always challenges me mentally and intellectually. He provokes me to pursue higher levels of theological processing. My sister Carolyn reminded me once of a word Uncle Cullen gave one day—"agora," which is Greek for marketplace. On that particular day he was telling me about Calvary, referring to it as the "ultimate" marketplace. He related it to something with which I could readily identify, invoking precious memories from my past. As a child, I would accompany my grandmother on her shopping trips to the food store. And man, could she shop! When she paid for her goods she was given S & H Green Stamps which she would later paste in stamp books. After collecting a sufficient number, she would redeem them for gifts at the redemption store.

Uncle Cullen told me Jesus did the same thing for us in lieu of punishment for our sins. He collected them all, took them to the marketplace—Calvary—and redeemed them. He exchanged His life for our sins, making us the recipients of redemption. Well, to tell the truth, I left the celebration that year consumed by these things my uncle told me, which gave birth to this song:

Redeemed

Calvary was the marketplace
Where Jesus purchased my sins
He struggled up the hill and had no money to give
But an old rugged cross was laid on Him
He exchanged His life for all of my sins
I've been redeemed by the precious blood of the Lamb

Although Jesus went to Calvary
And purchased ev'ry one of my sins
I still must bear a cross, if I expect to wear a crown
Had He not given Himself for me
I would not have life eternally
I've been redeemed by the precious blood of the Lamb

I've been redeemed by the precious blood of Jesus
He paid the price for my sins on Calvary
He gave His life for me and now
I have a right to the tree of life
I've been redeemed by the precious blood of the Lamb

Redeemed, redeemed, my soul has been redeemed
Washed in the blood, my soul has been redeemed
Saved, saved, my soul has been redeemed

The Battle is the Lord's

Then the Lord said to Cain, "where is your brother Abel?"
I don't know," he replied. "Am I my brother's keeper?"
Genesis 4:9

When you sin against your brothers in this way and wound their weak conscience, you sin against Christ.
1 Corinthians 8:12

The story you are about to read is true. The names have not been changed to expose the guilty. Just as the guilty are universal, so is "Kim."

This young lady, Kim, grew up in the church. She was literally born in the church, the third generation of a Christian family. As a baby, she lay in her mother's arms in the "cry room" on Sundays during worship. As a little girl she stomped her feet to the music in the pews next to her grandmother. By the time she reached her teens, Kim had established a lifestyle of worship.

She was typical in her development. She had the same experiences most normal children have—the same temptations, the same tests, except in one instance she was caught up in a story she invented about an abusive situation that happened to her. Her local church thought the problem had been alleviated. Her life's trials paralleled those of most young people. As the Scripture says, "All have sinned and fallen short of the glory of God." But the key question is how do we deal with others when they have fallen from grace?

Prior to marrying, Kim gave birth to a beautiful baby girl, a fourth generation baby girl given by God to be for His glory and honor. This child was showered with love from her parents, grandparents, church family and friends. Ironically, this became the root of the problem.

We cannot begin to know how Kim was affected by the stares, the remarks and abandonment even we, as church people can display to others. "Shooting the wounded" seems to be a gift of ours. God sends us blessings and then when we don't keep our eyes on Him, they become curses. Kim must have loved her daughter and saw her as a blessing, but something happened that wrote the scenario to a story, piano lessons, hugs from her loving grandmother for her daughter! These things were cut off from her at an early age; and so the story continues.

On the next day, feeling rejected, Kim took the baby to a bayou close to where she attended business school and left her there. What would cause a mother to do such a thing? We don't know, but God knows! The baby lay there asleep at the edge of the bayou. Kim did nothing about the guilt she must have felt. All we can ask is why? Why didn't her Sunday school teacher ask if she was her sister's keeper? Why did she come to church Sunday after Sunday and not get help? Why didn't she seek professional help? Why didn't a pew member extend koinonia and help her to connect with Jesus for deliverance? Why didn't an usher with the right countenance cause her to open up and tell her awful secret? Why didn't a choir member reach her with a song that Jesus is the answer?

Kim went along with everyone's assumption that someone had kidnapped the baby. Everyone in town speculated about what had happened. Days of searching for the child went with everyone wondering why someone would do a thing like this. Kim even passed out circulars and helped search for the baby.

The police suspected that there was a cover-up in the story, and at last, the façade was over. The deceit ended. Kim admitted that she left her baby at the edge of the bayou! What would her punishment be? What could be worse torture than going to school, knowing your baby was at the edge of the bayou? What punishment could fit the crime of knowing your precious baby woke up at the edge of the bayou where you left her, and in the darkness of the night had fallen into the water and drowned? Such innocence with such an end! And we are still asking, Why? Why God, why? Am I my brother's or sister's keeper? Do I have the strength to minister to such a need as Kim's? Can I try to ease the brokenhearted? Am I really so busy that I can't spend a little time each day ministering to some?

The legacy of Kim lives on, telling us we must try! Where is she now? In her own torment, trying to make sense out of a situation gone bad. How can we move beyond the shock of the situation to become "real" servants of God? How can we move beyond the pain long enough to help? We are our brother's and sister's keeper, caretakers of hearts too wounded, some would say, to survive.

The story goes on and finds me in the picture. I'd been asked to help with a fundraiser for Kim's defense fund. I was on my way to Shreveport, Louisiana when the Spirit overwhelmed me with "ramah", words from God for a specific need. The need, this time was great. What could I say to a family so torn with guilt, shame, and remorse? What words could God give me to minister to a young woman who killed the fruit of her very womb? I stopped at the convenience store to get the tools of the trade; paper and pencil, and began to write these words:

The Battle is the Lord's

There's no pain Jesus can't feel
No hurt He cannot heal
All things work according to His perfect will
No matter what you're going through
Remember God's just using you
For the battle is not yours
It's the Lord's

There's no sadness Jesus can't feel
No sorrow He cannot heal
All things work according to His perfect will
No matter what you're going through
For the battle is not yours
It's the Lord's

It's the Lord's...it's the Lord's
Hold your head up high...don't you cry
It's the Lord's
It's the Lord's...it's the Lord's
No matter what you're going through
Remember God's just using you
For the battle is not yours
It's the Lord's

The Good Shepherd

For he is our God and we are the people of his pasture
the flock under his care.
Psalm 95:7

Change is inevitable and sometimes difficult. It is non-discriminatory—it knows no race, creed or color. It has no regard for social class or status. It is inescapable and excludes no one. We grow older, moving from sunrise to sunset. We declare that things we once did we no longer do. But to tell the truth, some things we no longer do because we can't, which is a result of change. We start outdoing one thing, and end up doing something else. We relocate, going from place to place, and from pasture to pasture.

In December of 1987, while standing bewildered at a major crossroad in my life, I encountered colossal change. As a Christian I had to decide which road to choose, neither of which was detrimental. Doors that had been open for a long time began to close in my face. The parameters of my comfort zone closed in on me. God did not honor my desire, thus forcing change.

I had functioned as choir director and music minister for more than fifteen years at the Pleasant Grove Baptist Church. I loved that church in a special way. That is where I really began in music ministry. The people were like family and Pastor Charles Jackson was like my own father. They nurtured me with much prayer. They tolerated my humble beginning as a musician, a conductor, and a writer. But God spoke "change." I fearfully ignored His voice until He clearly said, "Enough!" My tenure there ended abruptly. The words confused, afraid, and angry don't bring justice to how badly my state had become. God had seemingly abandoned me. How could He have ignored my faithfulness to His call on my life?

During the month of January 1988 a miraculous thing happened. A group of singers called "The Redeemed Family" came to my rescue. They were organized to interpret the music that was flowing from God's heart through my pen. We had worshiped together in song for about ten years. We had grown together and had become accustomed to bearing each other's burden, feeling each other's pain and sharing each other's joy. Because of their love for me and our accountability to each other, we bonded with much prayer and study of God's Word in an effort to help me accept the painful change that I faced. That is when my healing began.

During a Friday night Bible study at my sister's house, Rudy White, a preacher friend taught from Luke 15 about the shepherd and the lost sheep. At the conclusion of his presentation, I was restored. A few days later I completed this text. I eagerly called my mentor, Margaret Douroux, to share the good news of my healing and the song entitled The Shepherd. She rejoiced with me, but after hearing the song, she advised, "Call Him the Good Shepherd...that separates Him from any other shepherd." Now I sing:

The Good Shepherd

Quietly He speaks to me
Gently He leads me
Lovingly the Shepherd carries me
He carries me hidden safely in His bosom
I feel His love inside when other times, my friend, I couldn't
He knows just what's best for me
The Good Shepherd knows
He knows just what I need!

Quietly He speaks...Gently He leads
Lovingly He carries me to safety
I feel His love...Gently inside of me
Jesus knows just what's best for me
The Good Shepherd knows just what I need

The Potter's House

Yet, O LORD, you are our Father. We are the clay;
you are the potter; we are all the work of your hand.
Isaiah 64:8

I grew up in a Christian home. My mother taught me values unique to that lifestyle. My extended family circle appeared "ideal" to me. My grandparents' lives reflected a type of perfection that is characteristic of transformed vessels living in the world but not of the world. Since they helped to rear me, I lived a protected life.

During my college years I left my grandparents' home and moved to Texas with my mother and sisters. Houston afforded many new possibilities, experiences and exposures. Some exposures were not as positive as others were, such as social drugs. I was prepared to avoid any personal involvement in them since I believed what my parents and grandparents told me about substance use and abuse leading down a road of destruction. I remembered the films I saw in high school about the consequences of drug abuse and this heightened my fear. Thank God for my innocence and naiveté! However, some of my friends and colleagues were not as fortunate.

Years passed before I became aware of great people within my circle of friends and the body of Christ who struggled with drug abuse. I saw frightened believers facing situations I could not understand, believe or handle. How could I have been so blind not to recognize what was happening around me until it was too late? Once my eyes were opened, I discovered this problem was greater than I imagined. However, the only means available to me to speak to it was a song, but I did not know any that could adequately address it. For ten months I prayerfully begged God for words to speak to my friends and ministry partners to free them from this stronghold. Finally, the Holy Spirit spoke words that would affect the lives of thousands.

Since the birth of this song, many have been healed. Please don't stop singing it, there are many more needing to hear it! The Holy Spirit trusted me to say to you:

The Potter's House

In case you have fallen by the wayside of life
Dreams and visions shattered, you're all broken inside
You don't have to stay in the shape that you're in
The Potter wants to put you back together again
Oh, the Potter wants to put you back together again

In case your situation has been turned upside down
All that you've accomplished is now on the ground
You don't have to stay in the shape that you're in
The Potter wants to put you back together again
Oh, the Potter wants to put you back together again

You who are broken, stop by the Potter's house
You who need mending, stop by the Potter's house
Give Him the fragments of your broken life, my friend
The Potter wants to put you back together again
Oh, the Potter wants to put you back together again

There's joy...in the Potter's house
There's peace...in the Potter's house
There's deliverance...in the Potter's house
There's salvation...in the Potter's house
Everything you need, in the Potter's house
The Potter wants to put you back together again
Oh, the Potter wants to put you back together again

Walk in the Light

You are the light of the world. A city built on a hill cannot be hid. No one after lighting a lamp puts it under the bushel basket, but on the lampstand, and it gives the light to all in the house. In the same way, let your light shine before others, so that they may see your good works and give glory to your Father in heaven.

Matthew 5:14-16

Dr. Bobby Jones, the one chosen for this age as a television host for gospel music lovers, organized an Artist/Industry Retreat a few years ago. It is usually held in Las Vegas, Nevada during the months of May and December. Its purpose is to provide a forum for gospel music personnel to voice and settle common sentiments and cares, find help for common needs and concerns, give directions to those pursuing a career in related gospel music areas, and document through the use of media, performances and seminars. I've been invited to speak at the retreat on several occasions. But the invitation that came for the December 2001 retreat requested that I teach a session on songwriting. In light of the September 11th dilemma, Dr. Jones also asked me write a song in dedication to the American Red Cross workers to teach at the general session. The request alone thrilled me. Every opportunity to express my passions about songwriting greatly overwhelms me. The thought of having the gift that lies within me on display in front of my peers excited me even the more. It was another opportunity for me to influence the minds of the twenty-first century Christian minstrels about the All-Knowing God. And I relished at the chance to speak words of encouragement to a wonderful group of supporters of humankind. The challenge was that I had only a week or so to create the song.

My approach to the gift of writing highly affects how I tend to use the gift. I believe that God has already planted within my heart, mind, and soul tools necessary to fulfill the call that He has on my life. That approach dispels any and all fear of completing any and all requests given, even when it comes from God through someone else. Since God, my Father, is All-Knowing, I have that type of quality within me. Since He is an Instant God, I too have that type of quality inside of me; ever since the moment He breathed in me the breath of life and I became a living soul. It is mine to access whatever quality I need whenever I need it. At times, the quality needed to finish a course is lying dormant within my soul, and the Holy Spirit so graciously awakens it on my behalf, just in time.

When contemplating what I would say in the content of the song, words began to flow with ease. Visuals of scenes from the 911 incident raced though my mind like warhorses. Flashbacks of many of the heroes offering aid to the wounded invaded my thoughts and clouded my vision. The words continued to flow. Their good deeds could never go unnoticed. God would not allow it. As the Father spoke through the Holy Spirit, I continued to write. Then the Holy matrimony between words and music took place. The ceremony was heartfelt and sincere.

By the time I arrived at the December 2001 Artist/Industry Retreat, the completed song was accompanied by an instrumental soundtrack. By the time I made the presentation, the

Holy Spirit had obviously gone before me to prepare the way. By the time we left the retreat, we all had witnessed the wonderful working power of the All-Knowing God in a unique way. Months later, the world had the same chance to experience the phenomenon as the session was aired repeatedly on the Word Network. Look at God!

Walk in the Light

Sometimes forgotten
Onward just the same
Unpleasant weather
Often in the rain
Determined to be faithful
To the call on your life
Everything will be all right
You just walk in the light!

Acquainted with sorrow
A friend to grief and pain
You look like God, Your Father
Even wearing His name
Guarded by His angels
Empowered with His might
Everything will be all right
You just walk in the light!

Denying yourself
For the sake of the cross
Sacrificing pleasures
To comfort the lost
Working through the day
Praying through the night

What's in Your Name

Therefore, God exalted him to the highest place
and gave him the name that is above every name,
that at the name of Jesus every knee should bow
in heaven and on earth and under the earth
and every tongue confess that Jesus Christ is Lord,
to the glory of God the Father.
Philippians 2:9-11

God-gifted individuals typically exercise their gifts at great expense to themselves. Some of the most profound sermons are lived before they are preached. The most powerful songs are born in the struggle of translating supernatural principles into natural applications.

Sometimes when I reflect on the movement of the Holy Spirit during the noteworthy days of my past, I can see how God works in the midst of the mundane. On one particular day, during a Fourth of July weekend, I received a CD produced by a Christian artist that included a remake of a secular song. I listened with trepidation at this song because it avoided mentioning Christian ideas of any sort. Internalizing the words did not give me any sense that the Holy Spirit had had a hand in writing them. I questioned why Christian artists would relive a text that is not Biblical, especially when the composers debase the Christ we believe in.

In response to my question, some of my friends said God

could anoint anything, whether it was created for His glory or not. After all, they said, He will ultimately receive the glory from all that we do. I pondered that thought to the point of questioning my own validity as a writer. Then I remembered the words of a preacher friend for whom I once worked. He said to "allow the Holy Spirit to get involved in your planning, then you can be assured He is evidenced in your performance."

Though I refused to grant credence to the secular writer's claim to determine what was correct for the sacred, I thought perhaps my time as a writer was fulfilled. I was devastated and sank into a spiritual depression. Books were all around me, including Bibles in my bedroom, as I sought resolution to this profound conflict. I frantically explored the words "sanctified" and "anointed." At the center of my confusion and disillusionment, God spoke to me. He told me that He sanctified individuals as vessels and not the vehicle. It sank into my spirit—God is more interested in sanctifying and anointing me, rather than my song or product. The song that caused so much intense inner conflict did not tell the world about Jesus Christ and His redemptive power. I was led to look at similar songs that avoided using the name Jesus Christ.

Not one descriptive phrase for the Lord—not "the Anointed One;" "the Man upstairs;" "the Son of God;" nor "the Holy One" —has the power of the name "Jesus Christ!" Should there be any doubt, I challenge my fellow composers and artists to forego advertising their names when they prepare to perform and to use descriptive phrases like "Anointed Singer," or "Gospel Performer," or "God's Chosen Vessel," and see what the impact of a name is.

At the end of this encounter with God, I wrote the words telling my story in the lyrics of this song:

What's In Your Name

What's in Your name...does it really matter
What's in Your name...who really cares
What's in Your name...will it make a difference
How dare we fail to call Your name

Though You are love...Your name's not lover
Though You're a friend...that's not Your name
Though You sit high...You're not the man upstairs
How dare we fail to call Your name

If I should witness...all o'er this land
To the poor...or royalty
No compromise...for worldly fame
I dare not fail to call Your name

Jesus...how sweet the name
Jesus...such a powerful name
That name Jesus...will make a difference
How dare we fail to call Your name

When the Music Stops

Be imitators of God, therefore, as dearly loved children and live a life of love just as Christ loved us and gave himself up for us as a fragrant offering and sacrifice to God.
Ephesians 5:1-2

A challenge is important for the creative. It is only when one is challenged that the opportunity to rise to the occasion exists, a time for the potential and the kinetic energies to unite. That's what I felt when leaving Sparrow Record Company's office in Nashville, Tennessee. The Potter's House was written and recorded. Signs of a successful marriage between song and artist had been established. A relationship between songwriter and record company was firmly established. The company's owner, Billy Ray Hearn, a trained Southern Baptist musician and former music minister, now a successful music industry executive, had invited me to Nashville. My assignment was to spend a couple of days at the office in the writing clinic and create songs. So I did!

Once I finished the assignment, Billy Ray and I sat in his office and listened to demos of the new songs and those written prior to my arrival. I intently watched his body language. Optimistically gearing myself up, I prepared to carefully evaluate his words. To my surprise, his words needed no dissecting. He responded without any hidden feelings. Words of approval were rolling off his lips like water when suddenly there was a change in his voice. He challenged me to write a song about what happens when church is over, once the choir has vacated the loft, once the benediction has been extended and the people of God depart from the sanctuary. I left Nashville feeling an eruption within my spirit.

Months passed before the second invitation from Sparrow was extended. Upon my arrival in Nashville, I possessed a degree of confidence that was not there during my first visit. The day passed quickly, culminating with Billy Ray and me sitting and listening. He honestly and satisfyingly responded to what he had heard. This time I challenged him. I proceeded to the little studio piano in his office and affectionately played and sang the song I had been challenged to write. I saw a metamorphosis take place in Billy Ray. At the hearing of the text and the sound of melody, the musician immediately supplanted the businessman. The respect for excellence in musicianship was absolute for him. The mood in the room overwhelmed both of us and we recognized the presence and work of the Holy Spirit. He yet inspires in creating that which the Father ultimately intends to be.

The real lesson in this story is that God does equip the believer and God does give gifts—completely. The Word of God should come alive in respect to our offerings back to Him. "I can do all things through Christ who strengthens me" then becomes a theme in the life of the receiver of every good and perfect gift. The Giver and the gift function best given the understanding of the recipient. The gift is what one perceives it to be. He, the Giver, is only who and what one perceives Him to be. I accepted the challenge, now ponder the song.

When the Music Stops

When the music stops...that's when I live my song
When the band goes home...that's when I live my song
When we've all said "Amen"
And the crowd begins to fade away
That's when I live the life that I sing about
In my song

If I sing a song of joy
I've lived it
If I sing a song of love
Oh, I've lived it
If I sing a song of peace
If I sing a song of happiness
I've got to live the life I sing about in my song

If I sing a song of pain
I've lived it
If I sing a song of despair
Oh, I've lived it
But God has given me a song of hope
He has given me a song of victory
I've got to live the life I sing about in my song

Everything will be all right
You just walk in the light!

Walk in the light
On the way to victory
Soon you will reign
In that Holy City
Keep your eyes on the mark
Soon you'll get the prize
Everything will be all right
You just walk in the light!

All rise!
Come seek the light!

Part II
The Proclaimed Truth

Introduction: Preparing the Way

By Margaret Douroux

The facet of Music Ministry that seems to be most subject to compromise is the facet of honest representation. The talent is usually genuine, the melodies are usually melodious, the rhythm is usually entertaining, and the theory is usually correct. In too many cases, though, songs written for worship say too little about the risen and the coming Christ. Too often does the objective of the composition used in worship seem to be designed to captivate and hold audiences rather than to testify to the goodness of God.

According to Deuteronomy 31:14, scripture chooses music as a major teaching and witnessing method. God's instruction in this passage is to write the sacred history down in the form of a song and say in that song that God is faithful to His people.

John the Baptist, who is known for his quest to prepare the way for the coming Christ, was challenged by his peers regarding this assignment. They wanted John to defend his posture in regards to the single message of a coming Messiah. John the Baptist refused to compromise his message and he explained simply that the objective of his assignment was to prepare the way for the coming Christ and not to bring notoriety to himself. His final response indicated that his position required him to decrease so that Christ could increase.

In this contemporary age, the new composer may be tempted to write for the audience, for the pastor, or even for the notoriety. In reality, these objectives may be appropriate in some assignments, but never in the worship song. The worship song must speak simultaneously with the Word of God. It must be strong in its conviction, it must be honest in its representation, it must preach of the coming Messiah, and it must not compromise.

God holds us accountable for our representation of Him, and because He does, we too must hold each other accountable for our offerings. As music ministers, we cannot accept weak, feeble, and frail compromise. Regardless of the era, the season, or even this new millennium, the worship song must stand in strength and in agreement with the Word of God.

Songs of the Proclaimed Truth

God speaks in many different ways; through His creation, through the lives of others, through situations and circumstances, and through His Word, either meditated or proclaimed.

These songs are the result of the Word whose podium is the pulpit, the place where life comes forth when God speaks to His people through His chosen vessels, the preachers. These songs are extensions of the Word which was proclaimed and then sung, with the composer as the person at the crossroad causing the Word to continue by the work of God's Spirit.

These songs were written during worship simultaneously with the preached word—they are "sermon songs."

A High Cost of Praise

It was the third hour when they crucified him...At the sixth hour darkness came over the whole land...and at the ninth hour Jesus cried out in a loud voice...
Mark 15:25, 33,34

It was Good Friday 1996. I had just finished leading the praise for the Brookhollow Church. Pastor Warren Stewart of Scottsdale, Arizona, was preaching a message called "The High Cost of Praise." It was a serious message; a heavy one and it pervaded the congregation like a thick cloud. It was obvious everyone had come under strong conviction as he talked about the crucifixion of Jesus. His tone was somber, moved along by a passionate appeal to the people to think about that day long ago on Calvary when Jesus was nailed to the cross. It was the third hour of the day, that is nine o'clock in the morning, when they pierced His hands and His feet and hung Him high. It was the sixth hour, or twelve noon, when darkness came upon the land as the Son of God hang dying in the darkness. Then, at the ninth hour, that is, three o'clock in the evening, there came the loud and piercing cry, "My God, my God, why have you forsaken Me?" Shortly thereafter, He hung His holy head and died.

The congregation sat riveted to their seats; all were silent except for those lightly audible sobs and quiet prayers that could be heard at intervals across the room. After a few moments, a handful of people, seemingly feeling some open response was expected, very nervously stood and began to applaud. Pastor Ralph West chided them mildly by saying, "The only proper response is Amen."

I was deeply impacted; I had such strong feelings and such conviction of heart that the words began to flow freely. I sat at the piano and began to sing this song—I had no written lyrics, no score, just the powerful anointing of the Holy Spirit ministering the preacher's words to my heart. The congregation responded just as spontaneously as we basked in the power of those words.

The following Sunday my sister, Carolyn, sang it at the tent services on the new grounds. Having written the lyrics, I taught them to the congregation and were we blessed again. I trust you will be blessed also.

A High Cost of Praise

At nine in the morning they crucified my Savior
Oh what an awful shame
At noon the sun refused to shine
The earth would take no blame
At three in the evening it is written that He said
Father, why have you forsaken Me?
Our wonderful Savior must have loved us so
Such a high cost of praise

At nine in the morning were you there on that Cross
Did anyone mock your name?
At noon did in darkness you begin to expire
In excruciating pain?
At three in the evening did anyone hear you say
That you were abandoned, left all alone
My crucified Savior died in our place
Such a high cost of praise

You and I should have been there on that cross
The wrong man was crucified
His life, His love for us He gave
Such a high cost of praise

Before I Tell Them

"...But only one thing is needed. Mary has chosen what is better, and it will not be taken away from her."
Luke 10:42

I was in Baytown, Texas in 1990 working with a choir during a revival service that was conducted by Reverend Charles Jackson, pastor of Houston's Pleasant Grove Baptist Church. I reflected on his message while driving home that night. I understood that if the Lord does not minister to the minister, then he or she cannot, in turn, minister to the people. Mary had chosen the better part—to sit at Jesus' feet and learn from him while Martha bustled about in the kitchen trying to serve without first being ministered to. During the night, I wrote this song.

The next day I called Pastor Jackson to thank him for inviting me to work with the choir. I told him what an impact his message had on me and that a song had grown out of it. He listened while I played it for him. He loved it.

The following Sunday I played it at The Church Without Walls. It was very effective as a prelude to Pastor Ralph West's sermon. It was to become the regular pre-sermon meditation for Pastor and people.

Before I Tell Them

Before I tell them
Lord, please tell me
Before I serve them
Lord, please serve me
How can I lead where I've not been
How can I show what I don't know
Before I tell them
Lord, please tell me

Before I teach them
Lord, please teach me
Before I reach them
Lord, please reach me
How can I lead where I've not been
How can I show what I don't know
Before I tell them
Lord, please tell me

Before I tell it my way
Tell it to me Your way
Please don't let the things that I do
Distract me from hearing a word from You
Before I tell them
Lord, please tell me

Behind the Curtain

Two men, Moses and Elijah, appeared in glorious splendor, talking with Jesus. They spoke about his departure, which he was about to bring to fulfillment at Jerusalem.
Luke 9:30-31

The Church Without Walls had completed the first phase of its building project and was making preparation to relocate to the new facility. Pastor Ralph West was preaching a series of messages designed to prepare the people's hearts for the transition. In his powerful message, "A Preview of a Coming Attraction," he helped us to see that the new building was symbolic of the believer's ultimate transition into the new and everlasting kingdom of God.

As Pastor West painted the picture of our great hope and expectation, my mind pictured what the heavenly scene must look like. In preparing the music for this joyous move, I replayed these images over and over in my mind. I imagined a stage with a beautiful curtain. The curtain was closed, and I mused on what one would find behind it. I imagined brilliant colors that would make the brightest hues of earth appear muted in comparison.

I thought about those who have walked across the stage of redemptive history since the beginning of time. I thought about Moses, and Elijah; about David and Ezra. I thought about all the prophets, priests and kings of the Old Testament era. I thought about the New Testament, about the apostles and the prophets and the preachers and teachers. I thought most of all about Jesus Christ Himself and what it would be like to finally see Him face to face. I thought about all those who believe on the Lord Jesus Christ through their word. We the staff and the family of The Church Without Walls diligently prepared for the transition to the Queenston facility. We joyfully planned the entrant service with excitement. I began to write songs specifically for the entrance. Upon completion of the text of songs, I asked Pastor West to select the song most befitting to this occasion. This song was one of the chosen. This song will always be sung as the entrance to the new heaven.

Behind the Curtain

A preview of a coming attraction
A foretaste of a final call
A glimpse that invoked my curiosity
A cast I can't wait to behold

A house, a seat, a reservation
A ticket stamped with blood
A King, a crown, a robe, a throne
A scene never seen before

A gathering at the river
A shadow of immortality
A sinner, healed, a promise fulfilled
A moment waiting for me

When I looked behind the curtain
The floor showed reflections of gold
The walls were textured with jasper
In the midst were great men of old
There stood Moses and Elijah
Saints as far as eyes could see
And when I heard the trump
I saw Jesus...there to welcome me

I'd Rather Be In a Storm

And they came to him, and awoke him, saying Master, master, we perish. Then he arose, and rebuked the wind and the raging of the water: and they ceased, and there was a calm

Luke 8: 24

Back in 1985, I was experiencing quite a transition in my life. I had been the Minister of Music in a large church, now I was in a more structured setting at Brentwood Baptist Church. I found myself a part of the staff. It was quite an adjustment. Even though the sanctuary wasn't as large, the grandness of the worship movement was always illumined by stained-glass windows, the crimson pews and carpet and the sermons deliberated by Dr. Joe Samuel Ratliff. It didn't take long for the choir to make the transition in becoming an integral part of the glory of spirit-filled worship—that is, praise and proclamation.

This one particular occasion I remember. He delivered a sermon entitled, "Riding in the Storm with Jesus". The point I remember most is...I'd rather be in a storm with Jesus than in a calm all by myself! The story about Jesus in the ship with His disciples placed us right there in the ship with them. We could see the waves dashed by the wind, the miracle of Peter walking on the water, the sea mist against our face.

That was one of several stories he rendered. In fact, one day, he expounded on when I think about the goodness of

Jesus, I can't help but thank Him. He went on to explain how "think" and "thank" are derived from the same root word. Dr. Ratliff was the third preacher I sat under regularly and depended upon for scriptural nourishment. The first was my grandfather, Rev. W. S. Washington; the second, Rev. C. L. Jackson and of course, thirdly, Dr. Joe S. Ratliff. He didn't fall short in bringing fresh manna from Heaven.

Later on, while still reflecting on the story we heard so much, and yet it seemed I'd heard it for the first time, I wrote these words:

I'd Rather Be In a Storm

I'm much too weak to make this journey all alone,
Every now and then I find myself in another storm,
I need help from someone who can calm the ocean down,
Oh, it is Jesus, He's the One who can save me
At the time when I'm about to drown

I'm not the one who turns still waters in a rage,
If I had my way, those clouds would never turn to gray,
I don't mind when my ship has been knocked
and tossed around
Oh, it is Jesus, He's the One who can save me
At the time when I'm about to drown

I would rather be in a storm,
I would rather be in a storm,
I would rather be in a storm with Jesus

I'm Still Here

But now thus saith the Lord that created thee, O Jacob, and he that formed thee, O Israel, fear not; for I have redeemed thee, I have called thee by thy name; thou art mine. When thou passest through the water, I will be with thee; and through the rivers, they shall not overflow thee: when thou walkest through the fire, thou shalt not be burned; neither shall the flame kindle upon thee

Isaiah 43: 1-2

The year was 1995. Pastor Maurice Watson of Omaha, Nebraska, was preaching a revival at The Church Without Walls (Brookhollow). His messages were powerful, coming across with boldness and clarity. His message one particular evening had a special impact on me. His subject was, "Tell the Devil I'm Still Here." This sermon captured my attention because it encouraged me to dialogue with the enemy, i.e., to tell the devil "I'm still here,"...that in spite of the enemy's fiery darts the Lord would cause me to be strong and enduring. I am indeed an overcomer.

I sensed the inspiration to tell other children of God that, " I'm still here. You're still here." After much contemplation and meditation on the sermon, I penned this song:

I'm Still Here

The enemy tried to destroy me
With fiery darts that I could not see
But God wouldn't let Him take me down
He sent angels, they've encamped all around

The enemy tried to drown me
Flooding my life with much misery
But God wouldn't let Him take me down
He rescued me to higher ground

The enemy tried to devour me
Clouding my path so I could not see
God wouldn't let him take me down
He lifted me to higher ground

I'm still here
I'm still here
I've made it through
So have you
Come through the fire
Come through the flood
I'm still here
I've been kept by His love

Nevertheless

We've worked hard all night and haven't caught anything.
Nevertheless, because you say, I will let down the nets.
Luke 5:5

It was Thursday night of the Progressive Baptist Convention's annual meeting in 1993 at the Houston Hyatt Regency Hotel. I had driven back to Houston from Waco, Texas, where I was conducting a workshop specifically for this particular service. Reverend A. Louis Patterson preached a powerful message that evening, out of which three points are stamped indelibly in my mind:

—God conquers
—God controls
—God changes anything

I saw my failures in light of my dependence on human logic and understanding. I had experienced setbacks, disappointments, and all of the other consequences of human effort without the Lord. But I began to understand the "nevertheless" principle. The blessedness was in remembering that God is in control and that even though I can't, God can. Better yet, He will!

This song was birthed in me that night.

Nevertheless

Time after time, I failed my test
Doing things my way, I must confess
Going in circles, out of control
Ignoring the good things I had been told
Oh, what a mess my life was in
No contentment, overshadowed by sin
Though I've been scarred by the world's wicked ways
In spite of it all, now I can say.

Nevertheless, God can

Therefore I, I am

God can conquer
God can control
God can change
Anything

No Walls

Day and night they prowl about on its walls; malice and abuse are within it. Destructive forces are at work in the city; threats and lies never leave its streets. If an enemy were insulting me, I could endure it; as if a foe were raising himself against me, I could hide from him. But it is you, a man like myself, my companion, my close friend, with whom I once enjoyed sweet fellowship as we walked with the throng at the house of God.

Psalm 55:10-14

I went to Brookhollow Baptist Church (now The Church Without Walls) in February of 1988. It was a young church, three or four months old. Services were held in the Brookhollow Marriot Hotel, in Houston, Texas.

I noticed a banner mounted on the wall behind the podium that read, "The Church Without Walls." I thought this was a rather curious slogan. Pastor Ralph West explained that the church would be on the cutting edge of the twenty-first century—reaching out to the total community and taking the message of Jesus Christ to all people regardless of race, creed, or status. The church adopted the following as its mission statement:

Brookhollow is committed to bringing men and women who do not have a personal relationship with Jesus Christ into fellowship with Him and into responsible church member through: equipping believers, enriching persons, evangelizing people and edifying missions.

I was greatly inspired by this. I understood then that the church is more than a building and more than an organization. It is a spiritual organism, a "living thing". It is the body of Christ making an impact in the lives of people.

Moreover, the Church is so transparent that the world can see what is happening within her walls. The walls are transparent so that the Church can see outwardly at the needs of people. Out of this idea came this song. I remember calling Pastor West on that following Wednesday to thank him for the Sunday worship experience, and to sing to him, over the telephone, the song the Holy Spirit had inspired. So now I sing it to the world:

No Walls

Walls can keep out the bad
But those same walls can keep out the good
Walls can protect you from the storm and rain
But those same walls can lock in pain
O Lord, no walls for me
They will restrict me from being free
To grow boundlessly
This church inside of me is built with...No walls

Walls can keep out your enemy
But those walls can keep out your friend
Walls can shield you from harm and danger
But those same walls can mar your soul within
O Lord, no walls for me
They will restrict me from being free
To grow boundlessly
This church inside of me is built with...No walls

Thank You for this building
That we've entered to worship You
Thank You for your children
Who've come so faithfully
Knock down walls of confusion
Knock down walls of disillusion

Knock down walls of deception
Knock down walls of rejection
O Lord, no walls for me
They will restrict me from being free
To grow boundlessly
This church inside of me is built with...No walls

O Lamb of God

And Jabez was more honourable than his brethren; and his mother called his name Jabez, saying, Because I bare him with sorrow. And Jabez called on the God of Israel, saying, Oh that thou wouldest bless me indeed, and enlarge my coast, and that thine hand might be with me, and that thou wouldest keep me from evil, that it may not grieve me! And God granted him that which he requested.

I Chronicles 4:9,10

In the Spring of 1992, Brookhollow Baptist Church had its annual revival. Pastor Ralph West, as well as the members anticipated this revival with excitement because the man he calls his father in the ministry, Dr. A. Louis Patterson, was to be the preacher for this event. The first night, the room was thick with expectancy as Dr. Patterson arrived. After the preliminaries, in his own eloquent way, he stood and began to speak. As usual, he resounded life-changing alliterations we will never forget. His text was in I Chronicles 4:9-10. He spoke about Jabez, "the son of pain," who was an honorable man. He related to us the fact that our name can shape us into what it says we are, if we let it. Yet, Jabez requested of God four things: 1) Lord, bless me, 2) Lord, increase my borders, 3) make me better and, 4) make me bolder. And God granted his request!

Jabez desired to move from being "the son of pain" to a man truly blessed of God. We praised God that night! I can remember how exuberant and full of joy the congregation was when we left. In retrospect, I see not only has the sermon blessed many, but the extension of the sermon in song, also. That night, I wrote "O Lamb Of God" and taught it to the choir the next night. On Tuesday night, we sang that song until the power of the Lord came down! Dr. Patterson was so elated, he praised God with us, appreciating all that God had done!

To this day, we say this prayer, knowing that we are inquiring of God something that is written in His Holy Word through the words of Jabez. We also hold the assurance when we pray this prayer, His Word does not return to Him void.

O Lamb of God

O Lamb of God
Bless me, bless me
O Lamb of God
Stretch me, stretch me
I beseech You, I beg You
I do implore You
Hallelujah
O Lamb of God I come

O Lamb of God
Make me better, I want to be better
O Lamb of God
Make me bolder, I want to be bolder
I beseech You, I beg You
I do implore You
Hallelujah
O Lamb of God I come

O Lord bless me
I need a blessing
O Lord stretch me
Increase my borders
O Lord make me better
I want to be better
O Lord make me bolder
I want to be bolder

Roof Tearer

Since they could not get him to Jesus because of the crowd, they made an opening in the roof above Jesus, and, after digging through it, lowered the mat the paralyzed man was lying on.
Mark 2:4

The year was 1996. Brookhollow Baptist Church was observing its annual Victory Celebration. We were celebrating what God had done through our church family and what He was yet going to do. We were preparing to make the move to our new facility. Pastor Freddie James Clark was there from St. Louis, preaching a powerful message from the gospel of Mark. He spoke about the needs of people and how the lame man's faithful friends brought him to Jesus. When they could not get in the door or the window because of the crowd, they took the roof off the house and lowered him down. He exhorted the church to step outside religious traditionalism to help someone. Pastor Clark chanted with a steady cadence and the congregation joined in:

Tear the roof off! Tear the roof off!

At the new site! At the new site!

I saw the picture he painted. Jesus was preaching. In the middle of His message, chips began to fall from the ceiling. The tiles, which comprised the roof, were pulled back and a gaping hole appeared. There! A man on a stretcher was being lowered into the room right in front of Jesus. The people declared that they had never seen anything like this before!

I was so greatly inspired by this message that I wrote this song:

Roof Tearer

I was carried by love ones to the house of the Lord
So that I might be healed
Though heavy I weighed, their love was much greater
Though afflicted, they wouldn't let me go
When they reached the door they couldn't get in
So that I might see the Lord
So they tore off the roof and dropped me through
That's when the Lord made me brand new

Roof tearer...raise your hand
Roof tearer...stand
Because of your faith for another
Love for your sister and your brother
Somebody's healed, roof tearer
Somebody's life been filled, roof tearer
And I've never seen it done like this before

The bed which I once laid upon
I'll ever carry upon my shoulder
To remind me of what the Lord has done
To let the whole world know
Where He's brought me from

Save the Boys

But the king spared Mephibosheth, the son of Jonathan the son of Saul, because of the Lord's oath that was between them, between David and Jonathan the son of Saul...
2 Samuel 7-14

I will always remember that Sunday morning at the Church Without Walls on Bingle Road in Houston, Texas. A printing company had previously occupied the modest little building that we then worshipped in. However, one could not tell that those walls were not originally built with praise in mind after experiencing a Sunday Morning Worship Service. The ceiling was low. Subsequently the choir and congregation sat on the same level. The pulpit was slightly elevated. The setting was rather intimate, capturing the essence of true worship.

Pastor Ralph D. West eventually stood with integrity and began his morning message. It was initiated by a quote from theologian, Harry D. Fosdick: The only thing that God can use to make man is a boy. The sermon entitled, Save The Boys, was full of useful information. The wealth of information in his sermon coupled with the real need to rescue the children in our churches and communities captured my full attention. It was then that I picked up a pen and paper and began to create as I listened to that powerful sermon. By the end of the message at that 8 a.m. Worship Service, the Holy Spirit had completed speaking words to the verse and chorus of a song. After completion of the lyrics, I charted the musical chords associated with the melody that was racing through my mind on another piece of paper. With Holy boldness, I handed the chart of music to the pianist, Stepheny Scott, and together we shared the song at the invitation. Only God could orchestrate such a moment through the lives of His people.

Still overwhelmed from having experienced God at the 8 a.m. Worship Service, I joyfully approached the 10 a.m. Morning Worship Service. We repeated the same format for each of the three Sunday Morning Services, by design. When the time came for Pastor West to preach, I anticipated the contents of his message. But, to my surprise, the Holy Spirit had not completed His work in me. By the end of the sermon He had ushered into my spirit words to a second verse. Is not that just like God? He pours more into our vessels as we empty them and again avail ourselves to Him. I sang the song after the sermon for both that service and the next. By the end of the next day I had completed the entire text.

This experience continuously reminds me of a truth about God. He is a right now God. It does not take Him long to do anything. It is me who needs time…time to prepare myself to receive the wonderful things that He has already spoken into existence.

It is His desire that ours boys are saved. He has granted both them and me time to work toward that end. Unfortunately, I do not know how much time remains, so join me now in an effort to Save The Boys.

Save The Boys

The only thing that God can use
...to make man is a boy
It matters not his name, his choice,
...it may be sports or toys
His value will increase
...as he grows closer to the day
When he leaves his parents' home
And goes on his merry way

Boys learn to love or hate
...as they are taught by me and you
With diligence let's teach them
...what the Lord has said to do
They're tomorrow's princes, they're presidents,
...our future's in their hands
Lord deliver them from sin
Only You change boys to men

The time is soon to come
...when this , Your world is in their hands
How can they ever make it
...unless they follow Your command
Lord, You made them in Your image
They've a right to be like You

Keep them shielded from destruction
Only You can see them through

Save the boys, Dear Lord
For they're Yours, Dear Lord
Raise them up in Your way
Fill their cups everyday
Impress Your Word deep in their hearts
Teach them Your love
Tell them, it will never depart
Save the boys, for they're Yours, Dear Lord

Speak for Me

Wherefore he is able also to save them to the uttermost that come unto God by him, seeing he ever liveth to make intercession for them
Hebrews 25:7

September 1996 marked an exciting time in my Christian life. I was serving at a growing church that was full of energy and new ventures. I expected powerful moments of Godly interactions on a weekly basis. This particular month was special for those of us in the fellowship because it marked the return of the pastor from his annual vacation and the beginning of the final quarter of church annual days (fall revival, pastors' anniversary, church anniversary), which was always explosive.

After the absence of the shepherd's voice for an entire month, I could barely wait to hear him again. Pastor West did not disappointment me. He initiated his return with a message about God being the righteous judge, challenging my very soul, yet offering me much hope. Interestingly, he answered questions in his sermon that I had intended to ask him upon his return. Isn't that just like God, faithfully assuring that the shepherd provides the right diet for the sheep.

During that following week, while yet pondering that sermon, I called Sylvester Turner, a fellow church member and attorney. I don't recall whether or not he was in attendance on that previous Sunday, however I questioned him concerning proper legal language in order to pen this text. He brought clarity to my thoughts and this song was born.

During the following month, we prepared this song and shared it as a tribute to the pastor on his anniversary day. With only one rehearsal, the Holy Spirit brought back to our remembrance the words, overwhelmed each singing minister with His power, and made known His presence to all who were present at that noon service as we worshiped with this praise.

Speak For Me

Regretting what I have done
Or what I did not do
I wore a painted face
To disguise the much disgrace
The quilt I then lived with
This world should not have known
How unhappy I was
Inside my now, sanctified soul

Remembering the day when guilt
Was taken away, erased
The thought causes me to shake
To think how my life was then
'Guilt' is no longer my name
The charges dropped, no blame
My God, the Righteous Judge
Pardoned my now, sanctified soul

Speak for me
Oh God, my Righteous Judge
Speak for me
Take my guilt away
Speak for me
Be my defense

God, my Judge
Speak for me

Intercede for me oh God, my Judge
Intercede for me
You're the only One I've ever needed
You are all I need
You know what to say and how to say it
You know what to say
Though I'm guilty You and You alone can
Take my guilt away
Tell them I'm forgiven and I'm given
Victory for my sin
Tell them all's forgotten charges dropped
The case is closed—Amen
God, my Judge
Speak for me

The Corinthian Song

But we have the treasure in clay jars, so that it may be made clear that this extraordinary power belongs to God and does not come from us. We are afflicted in every way, but not crushed; perplexed, but not driven to despair; persecuted, but not forsaken; struck down, but not destroyed; always carrying in the body the death of Jesus, so that the life of Jesus may also be made visible in our bodies.

2 Corinthians 4: 7-10

During late January 2002, I received a call from my friend and brother, Pastor Jimmy R. Miller. The sound of his voice alone brings joy to my soul. We often engage in wholesome dialogue peppered with integrity, daring to tread where most humans won't go. Our encounters are always propped up on the pivotal postures of our Christian characters. This conversation was no different. However, he was really calling me to invite me to share my gifts at a revival planned for the congregation where he served as a pastor. I eagerly accepted. I remembered our past. Each time that we shared in the same house of prayer, something powerful and miraculous happened. This time was no different.

The teacher for the three-night revival at Houston's First Shiloh Baptist Church was the pastor of Mount Corinth Baptist Church of Houston, Pastor A. Louis Patterson. The preacher for the revival was Pastor Steve Thurston of Chicago, IL. They were the other reasons why I could expect something powerful and miraculous. The first night, February 6th, was consummated with Pastor Patterson teaching from II Corinthians 4: 7-9. He broke the Bread of Life as though he had spoken personally with the Apostle Paul and God. I initially wrestled with myself, wondering whether I should write down what the Holy Spirit was dictating through Pastor Patterson, or just listen with the intentions of capturing and digesting every word coming out of his mouth. While suspended between the two desires, the Holy Spirit made the decision for me. I would do both. So I did!

The preacher/teacher tremendously blessed our hearts. Once he finished, Pastor Miller led the congregation in giving. That was a way of escape for me to go and complete what the Holy Spirit had started. I had previously noticed Kenneth Miles, a friend and fellow musician, sitting in the pews, who just happened to be the Music Minister at Mount Corinth Baptist Church. I imposed on him to join me in a back room of the building where we found an old piano. I taught him the music to the song that I had written during his pastor's lesson. Within a ten-minute period or less, we re-entered the sanctuary for the remaining service. I had to sing before Pastor Thurston's sermon. With holy boldness, lacking for fear of failure, accompanied by my friend at the piano, I sang this text. We all marveled at how God had orchestrated the movements of His worship. And we all knew for sure that Pastor Patterson had been in communion with God. I was just glad that I had walked, in obedience, to the Father.

It was inevitable that this song should be called *The Corinthian Song.* Its text evolves from II Corinthian and the preacher/teacher who inspired the song pastors at Mount Corinth Baptist Church. Hallelujah to the Lamb!

The Corinthian Song

I am troubled, yet not distressed,
Perplexed, but not in despair,
I'm a vessel, full of power,
With a treasure, none can compare!

Persecuted, but not forsaken,
Cast down, but not destroyed,
I'm a vessel, full of power,
With a treasure from the Lord!

Bruised and battered, but not broke,
Born in sin, but from sin I'm free,
I'm a vessel, full of power,
With a treasure hidden in me!

Thank You Father, for Your power,
It has resurrected me,
Over painful circumstances,
That my poor soul could not flee!

The Healer

And Jesus went about all Galilee, teaching in their synagogues, and preaching the gospel of the kingdom, and healing all manner of sickness and all manner of disease among the people. And his fame went throughout all Syria; and they brought unto him all sick people that were taken with divers diseases and torments, and those which were possessed with devils, and those which were lunatic, and those that had the palsy; and he healed them

Matthew 4:23-24

The timeliness of God can't be matched or measured. He does so many things at one time until the world's greatest minds cannot figure out how, when, or whether He is going to perform. Though He's a good God, at times He withholds His goodness when He has in mind a greater good. The time of the birth of this song text was during a span in my life when God had in mind for me a greater good. Pastor Ralph West announced to the congregation that we were approaching a study of God's truths about healing through a series of sermons and bible study sessions. The thought of what we experienced during that time in my Christian life will forever cause me to tremble. I don't believe those lessons can be matched. One thing I do know...they cannot be measured. The value in those sermons and lessons was and still is for a greater good. Moreover, they were and still are for my greater good!

My recall about some past experiences is as clear as the noonday's sun. The words that I recall hearing Pastor West say as he initiated this time of study were, "Healing is for everybody." That was enough Godly encouragement to take me from earth to Heaven. God knows when to say what through His Word. At a time when unexplained and incurable diseases had made their presence known to the world, God reminded us that He heals all and His healing power is available to all. So I told myself then and, with Godly pride, remind myself even while writing this statement of truth that I am healed!

Each round did get higher and higher as we continued the study. As the preacher preached I listened, the Holy Spirit inspired, and I wrote. But God had in mind for me a greater good when Pastor West shared four things about God in lieu of healing. They are so simple until they can be easily missed. Some Godly truths are so tucked away in the Word until we have to dig them out like precious pearls hidden in secret places of the oyster. Once we find them we discover that they were never hidden, just carefully tucked away until the perfect time had come for their discovery. So were the four points that I'm about to mention. God waited for the perfect time to reveal these profound truths to me. When He did, I did not hesitate to document them in a song so that the whole world would know that: 1) God knows 2) God cares 3) God is willing, and 4) God is able.

The secrets are no longer hidden. I invite you to share them with me. And together we can sing these truths.

The Healer

So you've entered into this building
You brought your burden and your pain
I have a message for you my friend
When you leave you won't be the same

So you've been to the physician
There's no change in your condition
Reach out and touch the Master's robe
There's healing for your body, mind and soul

God knows of your condition
He cares, you've got His attention
He is willing to make you whole
He is able, let Him have control

God can heal, He can deliver
He can mend your brokeness
He's got a miracle to fit your need
Can He trust you to receive

God has healed, He has delivered
He has mended my brokeness
He had a miracle to fit my need
Praise the Lord, I have received

By the time you leave this building
I trust you've got your healing
Once God's miracle has met your need
Go tell the world what you've received

The Glad'ning Stream

There is a river whose streams make glad the city of God, the holy place where the Most High dwells.
Psalm 46:4

The year was 1995. I was invited by my friend, Pastor Jimmy Miller, to share at a preacher's/musician's conference in Corpus Christi, Texas. Dr. Bob Wilson of Dallas, Texas was the nightly keynote speaker. His text on each night was taken from Psalm 46. He spoke of God as a vindicator. The messages were inspiring and theologically challenging. I found myself caught up on an intellectual high.

The audience was made up of senior theologians as well as academicians. I was especially aware of those who were seasoned in the Word and were able to think beyond the surface of a text. Dr. Wilson's messages were full of symbolism that this audience would understand. It was fascinating to see deeper insights and hear deeper truths in the Word of God. I became aware of the inexhaustible nature of the Word.

My thoughts were full of visions of violent earthquakes, volcanoes spewing molten lava, roaring waves and pounding surfs. The entire earth was moved by these cataclysmic events. Then my thoughts were transformed. Images of a great river pervaded my mind. Streams emanated from it, bringing peace to the City of God. Sensing profound serenity, and with much comtemplation, I penned these words:

The Glad'ning Stream

I see a stream...so full and free
Filled with joy...flowing with peace
And in the midst...God beckons me
To taste of sweet...serenity

Although troubled...today may be
Come tomorrow...peace waits for me
At break of dawn...His face I'll see
Then I will know...I'm near the stream

Just in case...you can't find me
I'll be somewhere...near the stream
Unveiled, though robed...with tranquility
In sweet communion...just God and me

There is a river...a stream thereof
It shall make glad...the city of God
That Holy Place...I love to trod
The glad'ning stream...the presence of God

Where's Your Lamb

Abraham answered, "God himself will provide the lamb for the burnt offering, my son."
Genesis 22:8

The year, I can't recall exactly. It was during the early 1980's for sure. Pleasant Grove Baptist Church was the place where this goods news fell on my hearing. Pastor Charles L. Jackson always provided the best that he possibly could for us in lieu of wholesome spiritual food. This particular day was no different. Hindsight has revealed so much to me about those days, those years. We had no clue to how valuable they really were at that time. God's Word was handled with so much dignity and integrity.

The spokesman for God had seemingly spent much time with God prior to approaching the sacred desk on that particular day. He was tall, young, and rather overwhelming with presence. To be from a small town in Texas, he had the flair of a city boy. But when he opened his mouth, the city boy flair disappeared, and his overwhelming presence was overshadowed by the powerful presence of the Holy Spirit. The Pleasant Grove family remembered his name, Rev. A. K. Haynes, from that day forward.

He told the story of Abraham and Isaac, father and son. And did he tell it. It was though he was there when it all happened. How could God relate such a story through someone so emphatically, yet was not there to witness the event? That's just like God. Though Pastor Haynes was not present when Abraham offered his son, Isaac, as a sacrifice, he was present for the Lamb of God to offer him to us as a sanctified servant. Though he knew not Abraham nor Isaac, he was well acquainted with the Sacrificed Lamb, Jesus Christ. It was evidenced in the beauty of holiness that he ushered into the house of God on that day. Abraham brought his son to sacrifice on the altar of God, so we were told. But then the question came…"Where's your lamb?"

I still remember. I will always remember. His sermon soon became our song. So I ask, "Where's your lamb?" And we still sing it. Even today!

Where's Your Lamb

Why don't I feel myself being riveted in the side
Why don't I feel the thorns being pressed upon my brow
Why don't I feel the nails being driven in my hands
The answer is in the precious blood of the Crucified Lamb

Where's your Lamb
Where's your Lamb
Where's your Lamb
Where's your sacrifice
Have you been washed in the blood
Of the One who gave His life
Have you been cleansed in the blood
Of the wounded Christ
Was it the precious blood of Jesus
That made the difference in your life
Where's your Lamb
Where's your Sacrifice

Jesus is my Lamb
He's my Lamb
He is my Lamb
He's my sacrifice
Yes I've been washed in the blood
Of the One who gave His life

Yes I've been cleansed in the blood
Of the Wounded Christ
It was the precious blood of Jesus
That made the difference in my life
He's my Lamb
He's my Sacrifice

Your Time Is Sure to Come

And when they wanted wine, the mother of Jesus saith unto him, They have no wine. Jesus saith unto her, Woman, what have I to do with thee? Mine hour is not yet come.
John 2:3-4

I heard the sermon that morning about Jesus turning water into wine at Brookhollow Baptist Church proclaimed by Pastor West, and it held my undivided attention. You know how it is, times of spiritual illumination. You've heard the scripture before, but all of a sudden its essence captured your mind. Encouraging sermons have a way of doing that! The timeliness guided by the Holy Spirit picks up God's people right when they need it. The woman who had the wedding did not want to be made a spectacle. The tension was mounting, as she appeared to Mary, the mother of Jesus. Would He do it? For some reason Mary knew He would never turn water into wine...but would He? In fact Jesus never said He would, but Mary told her, "Whatever He tells you to do, do it!"

The woman needed her moment of grace. Our vessels always need filling because there are voids of the heart that only the Creator can satisfy. We always stand in need of our moments of grace! But isn't that just like God to fill our vessels, not with water, but wine! The host said that she saved the best wine for last! When we think we've had great lives, with all the fineries of the world, here comes Jesus! He saves the best for last! His timing is always right and best. Satan wanted to make a spectacle of us, and God's immeasurable grace redeems us. Jesus filled the empty water pots with the best wine they ever had. When we taste the wine of His blessed presence, we know what we had before was just water...bland, tasteless!

That day, while hearing God's words of encouragement, I thought about how God's perfect timing of grace always comes to our rescue. The first two lines in the first two verses of the following song are the four points Reverend West used in his message.

Your Time Is Sure To Come

Even though you might have a problem
And have not yet been encouraged
Just do whatever Jesus tells you
For your time is sure to come

Even though you may not have walked with Him
for a long time
And have not seen Him work a miracle for you
Just do whatever Jesus tells you
For your time is sure to come

Fill your jars with water, O fill them
Then draw some out and take to the Master
Once He changes your water into wine
Then you'll know that your time is come

So for a life that's filled with
God's sweetness
Even though your vessels are bare
Just do whatever Jesus tells you
For your time is sure to come

PART III

The Mediated Truth

Introduction
Private Time with God

By Kathy McKay–Smith

In a world of fast food, microwave ovens, cell phones, and quick-fix methods, we neglect as God's children to take time with Him and meditate on His Word. David wrote about meditation in many of his psalms because it reaches the core of our being. Meditating is listening to God speak and pondering over what He has to say. It is taking every Word from God and letting it settle into the recesses of our souls until it comes alive within us.

In today's world, people use so many different methods to meditate, focus, and let what they are pondering on sink in. Yet what is the finished product? David said about the one who meditates day and night on the Word of God in Psalm 1, "He shall be like a tree planted by the rivers of water that brings forth fruit in his season." Those who meditate on God's Word, who let it submerge, know there is a reward. It is fellowship...sitting at the feet of Jesus, resting in His everlasting arms, knowing that He is ever near.

The result of mediating on God's Word is becoming God's messenger, having something to say to the lost, the forgotten, those who need a Word from the Lord. The songs that are in this section have great meaning because they reach the depths that only one who takes time with God can reach. Doing this takes great sacrifice because God never watches the clock. He may even want to talk to us in the wee hours of the morning when the world is asleep. And yet, when the world is not seeking God, there are always those who are listening; thirsting for His Word. These are His children who are hand chosen to perform His divine will in their lives; those who have allowed the meditation of God's Word to become an integral part of their lives. They explore God's Word, examine His precepts, and excel in the fullness of life.

Songs of the Mediated Truth

There are the quiet times—the retreats from my life's daily demands and routines teeming with activity and the stealing away into the sweetness of solitude—aloneness with the Holy One. I meditate on the Word of God; ponder it; reflect on it; focus on it to the exclusion of everything else.

God speaks to me through His word, telling me sacred secrets when I prayerfully sink into the depths of His thoughts. The beauty of God's Word is its inexhaustibility with regards to our questions about life.

When I meditated upon God's Word, the Holy Spirit's illumination gave birth to these songs, answering my questions about life.

"I don't know" is a powerful phrase.

All That God Said

The Lord shall establish thee an holy people unto himself, as he hath sworn unto thee, if thou shalt keep the commandments of the Lord thy God and walk in his ways. And all people of the earth shall see that thou art called by the name of the Lord; and they shall be afraid of thee. And the Lord shall make thee plenteous in goods, in the fruit of thy body, and in the fruit of thy cattle, and in the fruit of thy ground, in the land which the Lord sware unto thy fathers to give thee...

Deut. 28: 9-13

Lost I was...but now I'm saved
Bound I was...now no more chains
Washed in the blood of the Crucified Lamb
I am all that God said I am
I am all that God said I am

Once a sinner...but that's not my story
Bound for hell...now bound for Glory
Washed in the blood of the Crucified Lamb
I am all that God said I am
I am all that God said I am

Broken...but now I'm mended
Out...now apprehended

Washed in the blood of the Crucified Lamb
I am all that God said I am
I am all that God said I am

I am all that God said I am
Saved...sanctified...redeemed...washed clean
I am all that God said I am
Washed in the blood of the Crucified Lamb
I am all that God said I am

Affirmation

Now it is God who makes both of us and you stand firm in Christ. He anointed us, set his seal of ownership on us, and put his Spirit in our hearts as a deposit, guaranteeing what is to come.

2 Corinthians 1:22

I have an affirmation of who God is
My faith is strengthened more and more
Each day that I live
He whispers words of love that soothe my pain
Performs miracles I can't explain
Within my soul there's been a change
Through the blood of the Lamb
Through the blood of the Lamb

I have an affirmation of whose I am
My faith is firm, there's security
In the great "I Am"
The "Blameless One" has set me free
And for my sins He's pardoned me
I found solace there at Cal'vry's tree
Through the blood of the Lamb
Through the blood of the Lamb

Oh, oh, oh, oh
A new creature I am
Oh, oh, oh, oh
Through the blood of the Lamb
He washed me through and through
I've been transformed, made brand new
Through the blood of the Lamb
Through the blood of the Lamb

Anticipation

No longer will there be any curse. The throne of God and of the Lamb will be in the city, and his servants will serve Him. They will see His face, and His name will be on their foreheads.

Revelation 22:3-4

Can't wait to see Him...look upon His face
Bow down before Him...thank Him for His grace

Shake hands with the elders...the twenty and the four
Say hello to my loved ones...who've gone on before

Jesus is preparing...a place just for me
If you want to see me...in Heaven I will be

Time will be my friend...day will never end
Summer, winter, spring, or fall...won't have to come at all

Hope to see you there...where all the saints will be
Oh my friend...come and go with me

Calvary

When they came to the place called the Skull, there they crucified Him, along with the criminals—one on his right, and the other on his left.
Luke 23:33

I will always remember you, Calvary
Within your walls I met the Savior
Had you never existed
There would be no redemption
I will always remember you, Calvary

How could I ever forget you, Calvary
Within your gates my sins were forgiven
Had you never been lifted
There would be no resurrection
I will always remember you, Calvary

Calvary, I will never forget you
I rejoice the day that I met you
You showed me the way
To my Savior's bleeding side
I will always remember you, Calvary

Creator of the Valleys

The hand of the Lord was upon me there, and he said to me, "Get up and go out to the plain, and there I will speak to you."
Ezekiel 3:22

The earth and the fullness thereof
The whole world and they that dwell therein
Yet there's more my God will unfold
Mountains with hues of white, brown and green
Rivers with boundaries lined
Since God created the valleys
Surely, He understands mine

Perplexed, forsaken, forgotten
With troubles I stand face to face
When I'm feeling down
I remember the crown of thorns Jesus wore in my place
Despite my pain, I give thanks to the Father
The Creator of all, including time
Since God created the valleys
Surely, He understands mine

Valleys deep and wide
Reflect pain deep inside
Valleys shaded with gloom

Expose darkness in my room
But the Creator will take me through
In His own time
Since God created the valleys
Surely, He understands mine

Eagles' Wings

...but those who hope in the Lord will renew their strength. They will soar like wings eagles; they will run and not get weary, they will walk and not be faint.
Isaiah 40:31

Lord, mount me on the wings of an eagle
So I can fly above my situation
If I stay here too long...
I'll be consumed of my own weakness
Lord, mount me
So I can fly from where I am

Lord, mount me on the wings of an eagle
So I can fly above my circumstances
If I stay here too long...
I'll be consumed of my own weakness
Lord, mount me
So I can fly from where I am

On the wings of an eagle
I can fly above trouble
On her wings
I can fly above my stormy conditions
On her wings I can fly up to higher ground

On her wings I can fly above my darkest cloud
Lord, mount me
So I can fly from where I am

For Tomorrow

This is the day which the Lord hath made;
we will rejoice and be glad in it.
Psalm 118:24

Today is a good day
Today is a great day
Today is the first day of the rest of my life
I will live this day as if it is my last
For tomorrow is not promised to me

Today I have new hope
Today I have new grace
Today offers me another chance
I will live this day as if it is my last
For tomorrow is not promised to me

Why should I complain or feel sad
I will rejoice and be glad
I will celebrate Christ
The Giver of my life, this very day
For tomorrow is not promised to me

Grace

But God, who is rich in mercy, for his great love wherewith
he loved us, Even when we were dead in sins,
hath quickened us together with Christ,
(by grace ye are saved.)
Ephesians 2:4-5

There's something about the grace of God
That will ever be a mystery
It offers escape to the guilty
O what a mystery

There's something about the grace of God
That will ever be a mystery
It's a gift given to the unworthy
O what a mystery

Grace saved me when my verdict read guilty
Grace kept me when I couldn't keep myself
Grace will sustain me until I reach Glory
O what a mystery

I Have Fallen In Love With Jesus

And shewing mercy unto thousands of them that love me, and keep my commandments...
Exodus 20:6

Jesus said unto him, "Thou shalt love the Lord thy God with all they heart, and with all they soul, and with all thy mind. This is the first and great commandment...
Matthew 22: 37-38

I have fallen in love with Jesus
I have fallen in love with Him
And it keeps getting deeper and deeper
Oh what joy I'm feeling within
From the depths of my heart I adore Him
I'll let nothing come between
I have fallen in love with Jesus
I have fallen in love with Him

I can feel His presence all around me
At the time when I need Him the most
I can see His hand beckoning for me
O what joy His love does show
For my heart goes out to Him in earnest

I'll let nothing take His place
I have fallen in love with Jesus
I have fallen in love with Him

There's no doubt in my mind what I feel about Him
I really, really love Him
Deep down in my heart I adore Him
Nothing can separate me from this love of mine
I really, really love Him
O what a wonderful feeling
I feel for my Jesus
I have fallen in love with Him

In My Dream

Hope deferred makes the heart sick, but a longing
fulfilled is a tree of life.
Proverbs 13:12

I dreamed of a perfect place
With but one human race
There were no fears, no doubts, no tears
All hate had disappeared
I dreamed all men were free
There were no boundaries
No selfish pride...none criticized
All lived in harmony

No shades of black or white or brown
Poverty could not be found
The thought of men sleeping on the ground
Could never be In My Dream
This whole world is in God's hand
Every body, girl, woman, man
Instead of dreaming I should ask
What should I do...what is my task

To love you more each day
To help you find your way
To erase all hate...n'er intimidate

One with a different face
To give the best of me
To give unselfishly
This gift of love from up above
God let it be...as In My Dream

Just Like a Child

A child is known to say
All the things he hears grown folk say
A child is known to do
All the things he sees grown folk do
But a child is known to love
Even when love in return is not the same
A child is known to give
Even when giving seems to be in vain

If a grown man would say
All the things his Father says to say
If a grown man would do
All the things his Father says to do
Then a grown man could love
Even when love in return is not the same
Yes a grown man could give
Even when giving seems to be in vain

Unless you be just like a child
You cannot enter into the gates
Unless you be just like a child
You cannot see the Father's face
So humble yourself before it's too late
Meek and lowly is the way

Humble and holy is the way
Meek and lowly is the way
Just like a child

My Time

O my God, I trust in thee: let me not be ashamed, let not mine enemies triumph over me. Yea, let none that wait on thee be ashamed: let them be ashamed which transgress without cause
Psalm 25: 2-3

I waited for my time
I didn't get in a hurry
I waited for my time
I chose not to worry
Knowing everyday new mercies I see
Hand in hand with brand new possibilities
Unexpected blessings have been given to me
Since I waited for my time

I waited for my time
Not knowing what God had in store
I waited for my time
Not knowing when He'd open the door
But I knew He was always thinking of me
And I knew He'd soon come see about me
I've not time to tell all that He's done for me
Since I waited for my time

Though I anticipated, I patiently waited
For my God to come through
Jehovah Jireh, my provider
Always knows what to do
Like from water into wine
He's transformed this life of mine
Thank God I waited
Though I anticipated
Thank God I waited for my time

Removal Of The Mask

Then Jesus asked him, "What is your name?"
"My name is Legion," he replied, "for we are many."
Mark 5:8-9

There was a man behind a mask
Appearing to be whole
At the removal of the mask
Another man was then exposed
Fragmented and broken...full of pain and agony
Who relished the thought of being free

So he turned to the one
Who created every man
Just like a loving Father
God took him by his hand
One touch was enough...to satisfy his every need
I was that man...thank God I've been set free

In case you're trying to hide
What you're feeling deep inside
Deceiving yourself...by wearing a disguise
Let the power that's asleep
Be awakened and released
God will end the masquerade and set you free

I have a quality of omnipotence
Sleeping inside of me
It's been awakened by the One who created me
God's resurrecting power
Destroyed the mask that used to be
Now the man that you behold is truly me

Resurrection Day

Now if Christ be preached that he rose from the dead,
how say some among you that there is no resurrection of the
dead? But if there be no resurrection of the dead,
then is Christ not risen...And if Christ be not raised,
you faith is vain; ye are yet in your sins
1 Corinthians 15: 12-13, 17

I cannot lose, nor be defeated
Despite the suffering along the way
Jesus acquired my pain and trepidation
When He rose up from that awful grave

Forever, always, describes my future
Denouncing all that the world might say
My life can never, ever be aborted
A promise that cannot be taken away

It is not over 'til God says so
No matter what I may be going through
With Christ I live with this assurance
Knowing that He's done what none other can do

My life for Christ is absolute and certain
For the precious price He chose to pay
My heart now resounds with Hallelujah
All because of resurrection day

Since the Last Time

Since the last time I saw you
God has moved another mountain out of my way
Lead me to green pastures...turned my midnight into day
Placed my feet upon a rock to stay

Since the last time I saw you
God has calmed another raging storm in my life
Led me into safety...turned my darkness into light
Now I stand in the power of His might

Since the last time I saw you
God has worked another wondrous miracle for me
Led me into triumph...now my blinded eyes can see
That He alone performs victoriously

Since the last time I saw you
God has changed and re-arranged the plans that I made
Led me into freedom...I'm no longer a slave
To this work...but to Christ...my life I gave

You would have thought that God
had already done enough for me
When He took my place at Calvary
But He does more and more right before my eyes
I have no other choice but to stand and testify

Through the Storm

Immediately Jesus made the disciples get into the boat and go on ahead of him to the other side, while he dismissed the crowd. After he dismissed them, he went upon a mountainside by himself to pray. When evening came, he was there alone...

Matt: 14:22-23

The storms of life will blow
They're sure to come and go
They meet me at a time
When I'm calm and doing fine
But the Captain of my soul
Is always on board
He rocks me in His arms
While riding through the storm

I have no fear of the raging sea
Knowing Jesus is with me
He can speak to the winds and waves
And make them all behave
All power is in His hand
Whether on sea or on dry land
I've found safety in His arms
While riding through the storm

While riding through the storm
Jesus rocks me in His arms
I am not afraid of the stormy winds and waves
Though the tides become high
He holds me while I ride
I've found safety in the Master's arms
While riding through the storm

Turn It Loose

Let us therefore come boldly unto the throne of grace,
that we may obtain mercy, and find grace to help in time
of need....
Hebrews 4:16; 7:25

Wherefore his able also to save them to the uttermost
that come unto God by him, seeing he ever liveth to make
intercession for them....
Hebrews 7:25

So you've been looking for love in all the wrong places
Putting your trust in smiling faces
Failing to give up the wrong for the right
Losing the battle at the start of the fight

So you've been looking for something that will satisfy
Your needs, your cares, your heart's desire
Running in place and going nowhere
Choked up inside, can't even utter a prayer

Turn it loose...let it go
Give your life to God
He knows how to handle it
Get off that merry-go-round

Give your life to God
He'll take you to higher ground

Whatever you need is in the Lord
He's got what you've been looking for
If you make on step…He will make two
Let me tell you what you ought to do

When My House Became A Home

And he took them the same hour of the night,
and washed their stripes; and was baptized, he and all his,
straightway. And when he had brought them into his house,
he set meat before them, and rejoiced,
believing in God with all his house.
Acts 16: 33-34

Each room was filled with things
That had been gathered for years
Laughter filled the air
Seldom I saw a tear
But still there was something missing
At times I felt alone
Though I dwelled at this , my house
Still I felt I had no home

A portrait of the family
Was hanging on the wall
Sounds of happy voices
Leaped through columns standing tall
But still there was void
In this house where I lived

Though my parents offered much
Still one thing they could not give

When my house became a home
I rejoiced
When the hearts of family members…
had been changed
I rejoiced
When the walls had been saturated…
with praise to Jesus Christ
And the radiance of His presence…
filled each room with His marvelous light
When each family member said thank you…
By living a life for Jesus Christ
I rejoiced

Who Touched Me

There was a woman who'd been sick for twelve long years
She suffered many things...cried many tears
Spent all she had on earthly physicians
Got no better...worst grew her condition

She heard about Jesus and found Him in the crowd
From behind, the woman touched his shawl
That very moment...her affliction went away
she was healed on that very day

Immediately Jesus turned around in the crowd
Because of what He felt, the Master cried aloud
With fear and trembling, that woman fell at His feet
He said...Daughter, now go in peace

Jesus said
Who touched me...who touched me
I feel the power leaving me
Who touched me...admit it...who touched me
Go and tell somebody how He took your affliction away

Part IV
The Painful Truth

Introduction: The Wounded Healer

By Kenneth Edward Copeland

The birth of something beautiful often comes at a tremendous expense. Once born, however, that which is beautiful can become a timeless blessing. Many of the blessings we enjoy now have come to us as a result of someone else's willingness to suffer. In my opinion, the music of V. Michael McKay is one such blessing.

Much of V. Michael's music was birthed in him during sermonic moments. The Holy Spirit would inspire the preacher. The preacher would proclaim the Word. The Word would impregnate V. Michael's spirit. V. Michael would give birth to a psalm, a hymn, or a spiritual song. Sometimes the gestation period was a matter of minutes, and V. Michael would teach the song to the congregation at the conclusion of the sermon that inspired. At other times, the song was not ready for delivery until weeks or months later. That was how the process worked for a long season.

Over the past two or three years, my friend has made several major transitions. One of those transitions altered the customary process through which he birthed the music. In September of 1999, we had a conversation about the paradox of being wounded, yet still being used by God to effectuate healing. During the course of our conversation, I commented that perhaps his latest transition, though painful, was just God's way of drying up the brook. That comment caused him to immediately reflect upon a song that he wrote years ago that says, "Before the brook dries up, I've got to write another song about the same old story." As we continued to dialogue, the Holy Spirit made it abundantly clear that He was still speaking to and through V. Michael, though not through His familiar process. The old brook had not dried up. God was doing a new thing in order to enable our concept of Him to be even greater.

Two things fascinate me about the music God has expressed through V. Michael McKay. The music itself is timeless. There are pieces that he wrote twenty years ago that work today just as well as they did the day he wrote them. Twenty years from now, if the Lord delays His coming, we will still be singing the music. Equally as fascinating is the therapeutic nature of the music. It is difficult to sing this music without worshipping. For wounded souls, worship is the best therapy. In fact, the Greek word "therapeuo" can mean to heal, cure, or to worship. That is why the music is so curative; it's all about worship.

Mike, keep worshipping with all your might. For your songs are not only therapeutic for you, but they are also good for the healing of the nation as well.

Songs of the Painful Truth

These songs were written during a period in my life when I considered myself to be a mature Christian. It was a period when pain, in association with the birth of a song or songs, could be compared to the pains of childbirth. These songs are listed chronologically. As thought, they represent the trimesters of pregnancy.

Though the painful truth is told, God speaks through each story line and song. It is important the He shows up as the One who can and does ease all pain, who removes all pain, and brings joy out of all pain.

If the truth be told, I've learned to praise God even more for trusting me at this critical yet wonderful time in my life. He trusted me not to fail Him. He trusted me not to give up on Him. He trusted me to find Him in the midst of each painful situation. If the truth be told, He did not fail me, He did not give up on me, nor did he hide himself from me.

My Way

Surely God is good to Israel, to those who are pure in heart. But as for me, my feet had almost slipped; I had nearly lost my foothold. For I envied the arrogant when I saw the prosperity of the wicked.

Psalm 73:1-3

Early one night in July 1998, I had experienced God in a way that was totally overwhelming to me. It was as though I had actually seen God. The setting was The Riverside Church of New York. W. James Abbington was in concert in an organ series at the church. He skillfully performed literature of different styles, causing an awakening and arousing of God's Spirit in all who were present. Once he concluded, we were all drawn to our feet with applause of gratitude for what we had heard and felt. The applause was so great it ushered him back to the organ console. As an encore, he began to play the hymn tune..."Father I Stretch My Hands To Thee. " The skillfulness of this musician reconfirmed God's existence; but the sounds from the organ, the familiarity of the song text, coupled with the ambiance of the sanctuary, reconfirmed God's presence. Even the stained-glass windows, the large pillars, the carvings in the woodwork of the pews all reflected God. He was not only in the building, but He was also inside of me. He had totally consumed my being. My hands felt as though they rested in the hands of God Himself. My feet felt like wheels on a runway, awaiting a countdown for the take off—bound for Glory!

Once the out-of-body experience had ended, I marveled as the Senior Pastor of the Riverside Church, Dr. James Forbes, took me on a tour of the campus. Had I never known God, surely that guided tour would have been highly suggestive of His existence. Such grandeur, precision, and ultimate excellence in the application of wood, brick, and mortar could only be influenced through the mind of God. Walking where great men had walked, where celebrated theologians of past and present had studied, kept me reminded of the brilliance of the mind of God. I visited the private study where Harry Emerson Fosdick prepared his historical yet evangelistic sermons. I walked out on the balcony where he contemplated and viewed the harvest God had prepared for Him. To know that God had so orchestrated and facilitated the needs of His people decades ago through the construction of a building brought me into a deeper knowledge of Him as Jireh, the provider, the Only One who sees ahead. I began to view Him in a greater sense as the God of all people, despite ethnic, cultural, social, economic, and even theological differences.

Hours later, I found myself still reflecting what I had heard, seen and felt that evening at Riverside. The innate, yet mysteriously haunting thoughts of God's perfection, demonstrated in various ways, led me to an even stronger feeling of my innate inadequacies. Such a tremulous thought to view one's self through the eyes of the Perfect One! As Dr. Abbington and I later shared dinner with friends, I still could not erase the thoughts that had prefaced the evening. Once we departed, I still could not detach myself from those thoughts. As I encountered unfamiliar faces, walked in and out of unfamiliar places, trying to allow the sights and sounds of busy Manhattan to engulf me, I still could not abandon those thoughts. The city, Manhattan, was such a contradiction from the city, Heaven. The skyscrapers reminded me of the Tower of Babel, by design—robbing God of His glory. But then the Cathedrals reminded me of a place in that Holy City, whose steeples, by design...pointed toward Heaven. Finally, I surrendered to those thoughts, allowing the Holy Spirit to complete the work He had begun in me while at Riverside. I returned to my hotel room and allowed the Holy Spirit to birth that which was within me, using the faintest light possible. Maybe under a dim light all could not be exposed, I thought. Maybe if quietly approached, none would ever hear what I was compelled to say. Not even God! Nor even me!

Painfully I admitted that it was me who was speaking to God in that hymn tune earlier that evening. Though Dr. Abbington was seated at the console, it was really my voice crying out in that sanctuary to my God: "Father I stretch my hands to Thee No other help I know If Thou withdraw Thyself from me Whither shall I go!"

Though unashamed, I stood naked in the presence of God as He clothed me with another song. Though unashamed, I reveal myself to all who dare to read this text. Though unashamed, I will sing this song. The question is—can you sing it with me?

My Way

I've given up…I've made a choice
To live a life…that pleases the Lord
I wasted much…much too much time
Doing things my way
I cannot see…what's up the road
But thank God I know…what I left behind
I might not last…through another night
Doing things my way

To tell the truth…I must confess
God did not give me…what I deserve
0, but for grace—I should be gone
Doing things my way
What if the Lord…had come for me
Before I chose…integrity
Eternal life…would never be mine
Doing things my way

God transformed my thoughts…
and He renewed my mind
My feet had almost slipped…He caught me in time
Though I left my home…from me He never strayed
He yet regarded me
Doing things my way

Say Yes

Jesus said to her, "I am the resurrection and the life.
He who believes in me will live, even though he dies;
and whoever lives and believes in me will never die.
Do you believe this?" "Yes, Lord," she told him,
"I believe that you are the Christ...."
(John 11:25-27a)

My life had been pre-designed to serve the people of God at the local church level. I am convinced of that. After more than twenty-eight years service to the local church had expired, yet I am still comfortable as a servant to the people of God. With great joy, I embrace challenge after challenge. Seemingly, there was nothing too hard for God and me—in that order. For more than ten years, I had diligently worked toward the perfection of music as it relates to the worship experience. My consumption of this approach sometimes caused me ridicule, with statements such as... "Man, you've got a song for every occasion. " This consumption has led me to the publication of several volumes of music, designed specifically for the worship experience, prepared for the congregation to sing. At that time, I was Minister of Music at a local church in Houston, Texas. Weekly I planned music for the worship services. I not only planned the music, but also wrote songs tailored for that congregation.

Philosophically, I laid a foundation for worship through music for the congregation based on the following premise: "Songs should be relative to each period in worship, and relevant to the people within the congregation. "God honored my heart for this cause, and began to supply the substance to meet the needs to fulfill the mission, Frequently, I found myself thinking about worship and challenging myself to create by design, instead of by chance. God frequently honored my heart's desire, breathing texts and melodies befitting for the body of believers for which I served.

As a result of this process, all who were involved in the worship planning began to recognize, understand, and anticipate the accomplishment of this process. During the fall of 1998, 1 received a call from the secretary at the church advising me that the pastor was dissatisfied with my choice of song for the invitation. I attempted to replace the song, however, she further indicated to me that he did not want any of the songs previously sung. We settled for the song initially planned for that Sunday and I agreed to provide something different for the weeks to follow, Because of my dedication to the needs of music and worship, I took offense to the dissatisfaction of the pastor. I thought to myself, "How could it be that suddenly the song texts that had previously satisfied him no longer appeased him?"

In an attempt to gratify him and carry out his request, I prayerfully involved God in the search for songs endearing to my pastor. I remembered all the other times God had conquered even greater challenges. God then reminded me of words He had weekly spoken through the pastor during my years under his leadership. A playback of moments during the invitation began to resurface in my mind. The Holy Spirit began to rewind prior experiences of people literally running down the aisles during the invitation as the pastor gave the appeal. Audible sounds of the pastor's voice began to overwhelm me. His words began to revisit my mind, as though he was present. As the pastor spoke, I wrote. But as He, the Holy Spirit spoke, I wrote.

Say Yes

This is your day, this is your hour
This is the time for you to answer to the call
Can't you hear the Savior's voice?
Though He's waiting, it's your choice
Will you Say "Yes"...Say "Yes"
Will you Say "Yes" ...Say "Yes"

Without argument or debate
Question or dialogue
No need for further discussion
From your lips the truth must fall
Will you Say "Yes" to God's holiness,
Jesus and His righteousness?
Will you Say "Yes" ...Say "Yes"
Will you Say "Yes"...Say "Yes"

"Yes"..." Yes"..."Yes"
"Yes"..."Yes"..."Yes"

Silent Scream

The Lord is good to those whose hope is in Him,
to the one who seeks Him,
it is good to wait quietly for the salvation of the Lord.
Lamentations 3:25-26

Born the summer of 1998, this song was not publicly shared until six months later. Why? It is as unexplainable as trying to figure out God Himself. But I do know that He moves in His own time. I also know that He does as He pleases without any other's permission, not even mine. I once questioned Dr. Kenneth Ulmer, pastor of Faithful Central Full Gospel Baptist Church of Los Angeles, why an invitation to come and share with the congregation took so long. He responded quite prophetically, saying to me... "God had 'it' ready for us, but He had to get us ready for 'it'...and you were that 'it'."

Well, we were all 'it' on Friday night, January 15,1999, at The Church Without Walls in Houston, Texas, as Melanie Daniels of New York sang this text for the first time. Her treatment and passion for this song ignited fires within all who were present. I dare to say that only a heart of stone could have missed being 'it' that night. As she ministered, the Holy Spirit convicted me to ask gospel singer, Daryl Coley, to share the moment in song while simultaneously Daryl conferred with his wife that he must sing that song. Together they led all of us into a deeper knowledge of Jesus' sovereignty. Just for the records, the overwhelming power of the Holy Spirit identified another host of 'its' in Florida at Art Jones' Lake Yale Retreat just five months later.

While having lunch at one of Houston's restaurants I was introduced to an athlete/writer by a friend. He insisted that the two of us should engage in dialogue because of what we shared in common—writing. So we did. Periodic breakfast, lunch, and dinner dates followed. Intrinsic conversations became the norm for us. To know an athlete, a football player, externally strong, yet internally compassionate was great. As we continued our talks, we continued to unveil various commonalties. We both were full-time thinkers who spent quite a bit of time alone. We both had immense endearment for our mothers. Without excuse, we discussed our love for our moms at length, and how they fitted into each our lives. We began to comfortably exchange more notes about each other. I remember reading some of his writings and how astonished I was at the depths of his thoughts. He soon granted me the right to edit or re-work some of his writings. We would discuss them in detail. I began to know and understand more about him and his passions. I discovered he had a real passion for writing children stories, although not exclusively.

In a conversation one morning at Le Peep Restaurant on Westheimer in southwest Houston, while wearing a cast on his arm from a prior football injury, he read one of his writings out loud. Though it lacked structure, it did not lack content. Included in it were two words...silent scream. It was then that we began another clinical journey with words. The more we talked about those two words, the more restless I became. A familiar eruption began exploding within my spirit. Hopefully, my friend would not recognize the transformation of my countenance, I thought. I was quite uncomfortable with him knowing that I had been unmasked with words. What a travesty it would have been for him to know the truth about me. For at that very moment, those silent screams within me were trying to burst forth.

Finally, having to depart my friend's company availed me to surrender to my God's presence. God, without my permission, once again undressed me, leading me to a place of complete vulnerability. Having a need to resolve some of my inner conflict, the Holy Spirit began to intercede for me. He immediately came to my rescue, speaking on my behalf. He never abandoned me, but led me to a place of completeness. I knew then in a poignant way that the Sovereign One was setting me up, using me to bless His people. Why? For what reason would God undress me before the world, but for others to look at me, and by doing so, see themselves in His shadow? I love Him more for trusting me to represent Him in such a powerful manner. I love Him more for remaining true to His Word. In Psalm 94:9, David asks two questions of every believer..."He that planted the ear, shall he not hear? He that formed the eye, shall he not see?" I had to come clean before God in answering those questions. My screams have been heard. Hear what He breathed into my spirit and know that He too hears your screams!

Silent Scream

Dressed up on the outside
Things appearing well
Though you saw me through your natural eyes
One thing you could not tell
But the One who bore my pain
Fixed his eyes on the unseen
Jesus Christ, the Sovereign One
Heard my Silent Scream

How He ministered to me
Because of what He saw
While others judged me from the outside
He beheld my shattered heart
He then rejoined my broken pieces
Now with joy this song I sing
Jesus Christ, the Sovereign One
Heard my Silent Scream

Now who you see is who I am
All because of what He's done
I'm encouraged to ask of Jesus Christ
To point me to the ones
Who may be crying on the inside
Though unblemished they may seem

I'll point them to Jesus Christ, the Sovereign One
Who hears their Silent Scream

My voice echoed as if in the wilderness
Though millions gazed and passed me by
Perceived complete and flawless
No one heard my cries inside
But there's One who's always looking
At the unnoticed, behind the scene
Jesus Christ, the Sovereign One
Who hears my Silent Scream

The Other Part of Me

But whenever anyone turns to the Lord, the veil is taken away. Now the Lord is the Spirit, and where the Spirit of the Lord is, there is freedom. And we, who with unveiled faces, also reflect the Lord's glory, are being transformed into his likeness with ever—increasing glory, which comes from the Lord, who is the Spirit.

2 Corinthians 3:16-18

November of 1998 was filled with several trips in and out of Jackson, MS. I was involved with preparation for two different recording projects for Malaco Records, at the invitation of Jerry Mannery. The latter of the two projects was for a lady by the name, Lillian Lilly. I met her while rehearsing with The Mississippi Mass Choir. She was one of their sopranos. Though familiar with her powerful voice from previous recordings with Mississippi Mass, I never had the pleasure of personally meeting her. She was quite friendly and had a rather warm spirit. Her countenance was definitely that of child of God. Being a native of Louisiana, I felt that southern thing going on as we shared in conversation and in song. As a matter of fact, she nor Jerry appeared to have any hidden agendas. Both were genuinely good people who genuinely loved God. She played no tricks with her voice either, just stood flat-footed and sang. What she had was not a talent, but a gift from God.

Following one of the rehearsal sessions in Jackson with Lillian and the choir that was recording with her, Jerry and I carefully pondered over the content of the songs intended for her project. We rushed to the airport, as usual, trying not to arrive too late for my flight. I had already missed one flight while in Jackson and didn't want to gain a reputation for being a late bird. Jerry parked in front of the airport, and being the gentleman that he is, walked me inside. While running toward the security gate, we still discussed the songs for Lillian's project. I finally told him that I had not heard a signature piece, a testimonial type song for Lillian. He misunderstood me and responded..."She has a testimony. She had a twin sister to die recently." Whether or not he said more after that, I don't remember. We departed with 'good bye' and I quickly ran to the gate, barely entering the door before it closed. As I took my seat, those notable last words of Jerry began to stir up in my spirit. I never intended to insinuate that Lillian didn't have a testimony, but that I had not heard a song that would alone identify her. Though misunderstood, the Holy Spirit spoke words through Jerry that would influence the birth of a text to later influence thousands.

The flight from Jackson to Houston was about an hour and a half. By the time we landed, the restlessness in my spirit had been settled. I picked up my car from the parking lot and drove home with much anticipation. The thought of putting the music in my mind with the words that were spoken to me by the Holy Spirit caused me to stress. Finally, I arrived at my house, sat at the piano, pulled out the words I had written while on the plane, and began to play the melody that had been ringing in my head.

Seldom do I write songs for people or projects, but this time the process was proven different. This song was specifically for this lady and her project. I couldn't wait to tell Jerry what had happened. I remembered him telling me that he and his wife were going to a function on that evening, but I called hoping to find him back at home. Unfortunately, the answering service picked up, so I played and sang this text over the telephone.

Jerry and I finally spoke with each other the following Sunday morning. He then shared with me other interesting things concerning Lillian and her sister. The sister's death was sudden and without warning. The twin sister died a Jehovah's Witness, though Lillian is a Christian. The difference in religious beliefs caused tension between the two sisters, subsequently putting space in their relationship. I did not know these facts while writing this text. Another miracle had been performed. The Holy Spirit had orchestrated a symphony made up of players who knew very little about each other, but who knew much about their Father. Together, Jerry and I celebrated the wonderful work of the Holy Spirit. Though written with twin sisters in mind, all Christians can celebrate this theme.

The Other Part Of Me

There's a part of me, that I needed to be complete
So much so, I felt something was missing
In search for completeness, I fell At Jesus' feet
That's when I heard Him speak to me

He let me know, that He knew what I was feeling
And where I was, He'd been there long ago
While on the cross, He could see me kneeling
He chose to die, that I would know

He's the Other Part of me
That I need to be complete
My search is over, there's not another
Who could satisfy my needs
Now I can rest
Knowing I'll soon reign with the blessed
I can't wait to see
The Other Part of me

For Those Who Love The Lord

Peace be to the brethren, and love with faith, from God the Father and the Lord Jesus Christ. Grace be with all them that love our Lord Jesus Christ in sincerity. Amen
Ephesians 6:24

Consciously and subconsciously we tend to turn to those who share common thoughts and feelings during time of conflict, whether inner or otherwise. My life evolved in a way that eventually led me to a point of integrity. This integrity was initially incited within me concerning personal issues. However, some issues were difficult to face alone. As I depressed the replay button in my life, there appeared others who had carefully walked with me over tough terrains, through difficult valleys, and survived them all. We spoke the same language, bore the same pain, and fortunately shared common victories. As I reviewed my life's experiences, their faces kept showing up.

One inevitable truth or reality that was not easy for me to embrace was age. The aging process ushered in strange thoughts and emotions that were foreign to me. I soon realized that the only escape for these thoughts was to no longer exist. Upon this acknowledgment, I began to thank God for the most precious gift of all...life. As a believer, my thankfulness extended beyond life, but abundant life. He reminded me of this truth…"I have come that you might have life and have it more abundantly." The quality of life that God had favored me with warranted absolute gratitude.

As I began to reflect on the many blessings from God and considered the many years His faithfulness had prevailed, those same faces mentioned earlier kept creeping into my thoughts. Their voices rang on my sub-conscious. Words came forth like a mighty rushing wind. Even though the idea was fresh, I could here them singing. As I began to pen my thoughts, the tense for this text changed from first to third person. Seldom do I write a song specifically for a person or a group of people. This is one of the few times that the process had changed. This text is dedicated to The Redeemed Family, a group of singing ministers from Houston, TX. They have faithfully shared their lives and gifts with me for decades. Because of our individual and corporate love for God and obedience to Him, we are able to sing this text. These words are our words. These sentiments are our sentiments. This song is about our God!

And we know….

For Those Who Love The Lord

We've seen many mornings
We've seen many midnights
We've conquered many mountains
Thought too hard to climb
We've seen God work miracles
Throughout our lifetime
For those who love the Lord

We've seen many dawnings
We've seen many sunsets
We've crushed many burdens
Thought too hard to bear
We've seen God work wonders
And answer many prayers
For those who love the Lord

He's kept us through many dangers
We could and could not see
Some didn't make it...but by His grace
We' re here to testify

We have come to know just what the Lord will do
For those who love Him
Rest assured that there are benefits
For those who love the Lord
And we know just what the Lord will do
For those who will obey Him
Rest assured that there are blessings
For those who love the Lord

From a Distance

Thou art worthy, O Lord, to receive glory and honour and power, for thou hast created all things, and for thy pleasure they are and were created
Revelations 4:11

Isn't it so like God to order our steps and prepare our journey, even when we aren't trusting Him as we should? He leads us and guides us when the only thing we can see with anticipation is "down the road." Sometimes the "right now" journey is too much for us...so we look to the horizon for momentum! What I could see "down the road" is what led me to write this song. God knows when He needs to send us glimpses of tomorrow because today is long and hard. I asked myself, "Why should I be traveling this road now, Lord? I've seen and been here before! Didn't I learn the lessons I was supposed to learn? It seemed to me my "glory journey" had suddenly detoured and like Abraham, I was headed for a far country I knew nothing about. I asked God again about the lessons I thought I had learned. Really, I was always counseling with someone on how to walk in obedience as a minister of music! How could this be happening to me? And God answered me saying, "You can always grow in the matter of trust! There is always room for improvement in the area of faith."

I had to admit there is something about growing accustomed to certain trials that give you a certain edge! The pitfalls, you've seen them before; the enemy is using his same old tricks, which you've already experienced. How could I be leaving another work environment again after giving so much of myself? How could I be looking to starting all over again in a new worship environment? As I began to ask myself these questions, the fog dissipated. I looked up and from a distance, I could see glory! Glory calls those who work diligently for the Lord, because glory holds our reward. At that time, through my tears of despair, I needed to see glory! In the living of these days, I know now I must look up and see, look forward and dream, press on and survive.

Traveling this pathway lately has taken me to places I thought were further down the road. Things I held dear have been taken away before I thought I was ready, those crutches have been snatched way...but still I must press on. This song encourages me to travel on, even when the smallest step is overwhelming and exhausting.

I picked up my pen that day. It was a time filled with unanswered questions and misunderstood whispers. Yet, in the midst of those troubled times, I wrote:

From a Distance

I traveled far...on my way home
At times...I thought I'd lost my way
Finally...a shadow of Heaven...Heaven
From a distance...became clear to me

I saw millions...standing at her gates
As I drew closer...pressing my way
Finally...a shadow of my Savior... Jesus
From a distance...became clear to me

From a distance...I could see Glory
From a distance...I heard Angels crying "Holy"
What was once a dream...had become reality
From a distance...it became clear to me

I Call Him Jesus Christ

Jesus and his disciples went on to the villages around Caesarea Philippi. On the way he asked them, "Who do people say I am?" They replied, "Some say John the Baptist, others say Elijah, and still others, one of the prophets." "But what about you?" he asked. "Who do you say I am?" Peter answered, "You are the Christ." Jesus warned them not to tell anyone about him.

Mark 8:27-30

It was a cool Friday night...much like others we had experienced when we attended musicals, yet I didn't know why we couldn't sense the thrill in the air. Collegians were milling around preparing to display an extravaganza of dancing, stomping, and clapping, mesmerizing the crowd with their festivity?

The program began and all the groups present represented with their talent. We thought they had exhausted their energy, we thought the audience was tired, we thought there was nowhere else God could take us... and were we wrong! Have you ever seen a song explode like a flower in bloom, each stage revealing more and more about the glory of God? It happened that night!

The song, *I Call Him Jesus Christ* came from much agony and yet, the glory exceeded the agony! I wrote it at a time in my life when I began to see Christ manifest Himself among a backdrop of doubt and fear. I don't know, really which is the greatest...fear or doubt...but I do know both were at work in my life-fear of tomorrow and doubt of things to come. Jesus, who desires to give us the abundant life, even in the midst of trouble, began to exceed my imagination with his boundless character. As I would realize one character, another would show up! He is able to do exceedingly abundantly above all that we can ask or THINK! Now back to the performance on that night. The choir was above expectation and the Holy Spirit was at work. The song crescendoed in a mind-boggling sort of way just as the experience of naming Christ overwhelms us!

When does Christ reveal Himself to us more, I think it's when we praise Him! As we become open through praise, the Holy Spirit speaks to our souls and lets us see Christ clearer! Are we superhuman to the extent we never experience doubt or fear? Even the disciples on the boat with Jesus present had their existence overshadowed with both. Christ always manifests Himself in ways to answer our questions...We ask: Jesus, can you heal me? He says, "I am Jehovah-Rapha!" Jesus, can you deliver me? He says, "I am Jehovah-Sabboth!" Jesus, can you give me peace? He says, "I am Jehovah-Shalom!" The awakenings of who Jesus is grows more and more extensive as He challenges our doubts and fears with Himself. It WAS Jesus who said, "I am Alpha and Omega, the Beginning and the End!"

I Call Him Jesus Christ

Jesus, I call him Jesus Christ
He's the keeper of my life
He came to set me free
To loose the chains that were holding me
That's who He is, and what He's done for me

He is the One who saved me
And put His sweet Spirit down in me
At times I wonder what to call Him
The One who keeps on doing great things for me
When I call Him Savior
He shows up as my Comforter
It confounds me just what to call Him
The One who keeps on doing great things for me

He is the One who made me
And with His great power, He raised me
At times I wonder what to call Him
The One who keeps on doing great things for me
When I call Him Creator
He shows up as my Lifter
It confounds me just what to call Him
The One who keeps on doing great things for me

I call Him as I know Him
The Holy Spirit continuously shows me
He reveals to me
Opens my eyes so that I might see
Just who He is and what He's done for me

Thank You Jesus for who You are
And what You've done for me

Tell Me
(I Need A Word)

Then Saul drew near to Samuel in the gate, and said, "Tell me I pray thee, where the seer's house is." And Samuel answered Saul and said, "I am the seer: go up before me unto the high place; for ye shall eat with me today, and tomorrow I will let thee go and will tell thee all that is in thine heart..." And as they were going down to the end of the city, Samuel said to Saul, "Bid the servant pass on before us, (and he passed on,) but stand thou still a while, that I may shew thee the word of God."

1 Samuel 9:18-27

All alone, isolated, secluded, and needing encouragement, best describes my spiritual posture during the spring of 1999. Feeling as though I had failed God and others entered periodically into my mind. Difficult decisions stared me in my face. I was again at a crossroad, wondering which route to take, only to notice God's hand, explicitly pointing the way. Seemingly, no one else could see His hand. Probably no one else should have seen it. After all, He was specifically plotting out the way for me. I'm sure He was most concerned with me confirming my trust and obedience toward Him. Some decisions did not imply questions of right or wrong, but my will to do as God had instructed. There were other indicators of the degree of my personal trust in Him. Time soon became a factor in measuring my trust. The familiar inquest surfaced..."How long must I stay here? " I knew from past experiences to wait on God. Still, ' ole man doubt' found my address. Watching everyone and everything around me prosper, while waiting on God, then caused stress. Another trick of the enemy was attempted to deter my trust away from God. However, in the midst of all those distractions, I still saw God's hand beckoning for me.

The enemy seldom works alone. He uses whomever he can. Rev. Charles L. Jackson, pastor of Pleasant Grove Baptist Church, Houston, Texas, warned us of the enemy years ago, referring to his helpers as "his little imps." They emerge unexpectedly, frequently in the unexpected. Friends and family members began to express thoughts and beliefs that spoke discouragement to me. I couldn't hold that against them, so..."I charged it to their heads and not their hearts. " They said things hoping to encourage me, yet were in opposition to God's divine plan for my life. Because of our relationship and the uniqueness of our rapport, there were times I was tempted to believe their report. Before long, I remembered God's hand, eradicating all temptation. Unfortunately, none of my friends and family members were present when God spoke direction in my life. If they knew better, they would have spoke differently. How could I hold them accountable for what they did not know?

In an effort to escape those other voices, whether of friends, family members, or foes, solitude became my resolve. I found refuge in loneliness. The absence of interference from mortal beings allowed me to give God my full attention. His Word invaded my thoughts. Once my behavior was totally controlled by His Word, others perceived me to be somewhat aloof or detached from reality. But the Holy Spirit's voice resounded clearly, reminding me who I am and whose I am. The Spirit began to recall messages previously deposited within me. He brought back to my remembrance "all of the good things God had done. " Then I began to talk to myself. While in solitude, I spoke to myself in a manner that would make my Father proud having me as His child, knowing He was listening. Thank God I not only knew of Him, but I knew Him. I knew His Word.

This was another critical period in my life when the only thing that could suit or satisfy my situation was His Word. I survived off the indwelling of His Word within me. Subsequently, a change in my state of being took place. My conversation changed! My countenance changed! Others around me changed their perception of what God was doing with, to, and through me.

It was at this place in my life that the manifestation of God's gift to me was again displayed through a song. I can't tell you of the joy I felt in knowing that God could trust me to obey Him and use me to boast in the beauty of His Word!

Tell Me!
(I Need A Word)

Tell me
I need a Word
Tell me what you know
Not just what you heard
One Word from the Father
Will carry me through
Please tell me
I'm depending on you
Don't keep it to yourself
I'm standing in need of your help
Tell me

Word
A lamp for my feet, a light for my path
That's the Word
Something sharper than a two-edged sword
That's the Word
Something I can hide deep down in my heart
That's the Word
Word

I am Praying for You

For who among men knows the thoughts of a man except the man's spirit within him? In the same way no one knows the thoughts of God except the Spirit of God.
1 Corinthians 2:11

Uncle John, my mentor, my friend...left me at a time when I most needed him. He could always communicate to me and make sense of the moment. He had a special way of encouraging that was so unique and effective. After many years of suffering, he went to Glory. Brokenhearted, I began writing this song immediately after his death before his home going service, but the Holy Spirit didn't complete it until June of '99, the following month.

His wife, my Aunt Christine, had always been the Rock of Gibraltar. I had seen her weather storms and confront disappointment, but this time was different. The urgency I felt to complete this song was motivated by a need to speak to her to the point of healing. She was in anguish and I knew, like countless other song texts, the Holy Spirit was the only One who could speak to her and lead her down the road of healing. I heard her verbalize her pain and even though my arms were around her, I felt helpless to minister to her excruciating pain.

Even when we practiced the song, her daughter, Camille, would weep. Other members of the Redeemed Family would also weep, as it ministered to them. Some of them, they told me, would play the tape of the rehearsal over and over and sing along and pray for members of their family, too, who needed intercession. We were rehearsing to sing in concert in Tampa, Florida at Dr. Art Jones' church. What a time to be ministering...when we needed so much ministering to ourselves! We left for Florida with many mishaps and yet, God was working all the time. The Friday we arrived was overwhelming spiritually because the song ministered so in service (I mean rehearsal). No, it was a service, a healing service. I had already received an inkling of the level of ministry of this song, but during that rehearsal, I began to really understand.

The following Sunday was no different. At the concert, I called Aunt Chris up front and Hope Luster, the soloist, began to sing with such a soothing sound! People began to weep, to shout, to cry out to God and we all were blessed, the Body of Christ, the Family of God, the Redeemed Family, the families present. There is strength in unity! The intention of God is that we bond together in Christian love, the strong bearing the infirmity of the weak and those who can rejoice pausing to weep with those who weep. The power unleashed in this song will never be forgotten by those present. I, too, remember and await with "holy anxiety" the things to come.

This song speaks of the power of intercession, leading those to intercede and approach the throne of God for those who cannot pray for themselves. Like the boy with the fish and the loaves of bread, I thought what I had was only for a few, but it ended up ministering to the multitude. I praise God for appointing me these words:

I Am Praying for You

To the one who may be going through
The one who don't know what to do
I'm praying...praying for you
The One who I am praying to
Is the One who knows what's best for you
I'm praying...praying for you
He knows your heart is heavy
To Him that really matters
In time He'll make things better
So remember...family member
I'm praying for you

To the one who may be feeling low
The one who don't know where to go
I'm praying...praying for you
The One who I am praying to
Is the One who loves and cares for you
I'm praying...praying for you
How it breaks His heart
Just to see you cry
In time He'll wipe your weeping eyes
So remember...family member
I'm praying for you

I am praying...praying for you
I am praying...until you get your breakthrough
I'm gonna tell God about you
Call you by your name
Before you even know it
Things are gonna change
He's gonna lift your burden
Lighten up your load
Yokes will be broken
You'll come shining like pure gold
You're gonna tell everybody
What the Lord has done
How He's made the difference
Where He's brought you from
For the One I'm praying to
Is the One who'll see you through
So remember...family member
I'm praying for you

The One Who's Always Looking

As the heart panteth after the water brooks,
so panteth my soul after thee, O God. My soul thirsteth
for God, for the living God: when shall I come and appear
before God?
Psalm 42: 1-2

Self-evaluation can sometimes be painful and downright difficult. "When the music stops," "When the band goes home, " or the time spent with myself has proven to be somewhat agonizing. Why? Maybe I am severely critical of myself. Maybe I'm never satisfied with who I am and what I see. Is it that I'm that bad of a person? Do I fall that short? Maybe I'm ashamed or embarrassed of who and what I am because of what I know to be true about myself. The one in the mirror has always been the most difficult to honestly face-off with, whom I'll refer to as 'my friend.' 'My friend' never lies, but is the one who reflects the real person, showing the real scars, pains, wounds, and flaws. That's the one who also reflects the victories, achievements, and triumphs. 'My friend' is always there. Wherever I am, so is 'my friend', knowing all of my deepest secrets. Even those things shared by others, though asked not to tell, no matter how confidential or personal, 'my friend' knows. 'My friend' is also aware of the vows that I've made in times past. That's who stood with me, even when I committed my life to Christ, hearing all that I promised then...knowing whether or not I've been faithful since.

The dilemma in facing off with one's self is directly connected to truth. I'm guilty of attempting to shape or reshape the truth in order to satisfy myself. This truth is according to the Word of God, which is absolute. I remember the late Pastor Freddie Dunn of New Orleans, La., saying..."It's the truth, and it's in your bible. If you don't like it, tear it out." His sarcasm was rather humorous, but powerful. In other words, one is not compelled to appreciate or believe the truth, according to the Word of God, to the extent of tearing its contents out of the bible, but that does not affect, alter, or discount its veracity. Once I surrendered to the truth about who and what I am, in light of God's Word, I made some awesome discoveries. Despite my faults and failures, my Father loves me. In view of all my imperfections, shortcomings, and plain old sins, I am forgiven by my Father. He does not see me condemned! He sees me pardoned! God's grace is sufficient! Though undeserving, He does not expose me to the world, but I'm grateful He exposes all of me to me. Moreover, I'm most gracious to Him for not allowing me to become comfortable in my sin. Because of His love for me, He causes uneasiness within my spirit. As long as I'm vexed, agitated, annoyed, and disturbed on the inside, with respect to my sin, I'm reminded that my Father is still working on me. My hope lies in the fact that in His own time, my change will come! In His own time, both me and 'my friend' will mirror His face! This truth, I know for sure! The birth of this text was summoned through painful, yet intended self-evaluation. Born in the spring of 1999, while moving in the direction of personal healing, this was one of the stations by which I had to stop. There was no way around it. It was totally unavoidable.

At this station, I discovered three persons present. There 'I' stood. There stood 'my friend,' the one in the mirror. But finally, there stood, hovering over the both of us, 'God,' my Creator.

The One Who's Always Looking

Every now and then I look in the mirror
I dare to talk to myself
Knowing no one's in the middle
Distracting me with counterfeit help
That's the time reserved just for me
To get real and deal honestly
With the one who I see
And the One who's always looking at me

Sometimes I cry because of what I see
As God's light shines on me
Exposing all my faults and my failures
But then I stop long enough to remember
He has blotted out all my transgressions
I was reminded while at true confessions
With the one I see
And the One who's always looking at me

He's always lookin'
No matter where I go
I cannot hide from Him
He's always bookin'
No matter what I do

Even when I'm hookin' and crookin'
He sees…but I'm glad
He knows...how to hold a secret
He gives...me strength
In time...to overcome my weakness
Now I know what it means to be free
To live in sweet harmony
With the one who I see
And the One who's always looking at me

You Are Worthy

And I beheld, and I heard the voice of many angels round about the throne and the beasts and the elders: and the number of them was ten thousand times ten thousand and thousands of thousands. Saying with a loud voice, Worthy is the Lamb that was slain to receive power, and riches, and wisdom, and strength, and honour, and glory, and blessing.

Revelation 5:11-12

At the point of embarking upon the end of thirty years leading God's people in worship, I began to question not my own life's priorities...but the process! It seemed the road to giving God glory was filled with detour signs, crossroads and even stop signs, when I needed to be still and know that God is God. I also began to pray and ask God when would it all change and He helped me see it may never change, but the charge remains...to give Him glory with all that is within me. My own unique charge is to lead worshippers to glorify God by opening up their hearts to all that He is. An open heart is like a blossomed flower that reveals what is inside as it strives to reach the sun. Worshipping is our way, with the help of His Spirit, to let the world see what is inside us as we open up to the Son, Jesus Christ! Hopefully, when they see us appreciate brand new mercies on a brand new day, the simple pleasures of life, it motivates them to join us in praising the Giver of every good and perfect gift.

The greatest forces within us are not our uncertainties, but affirmations leading to the premise, no matter what, God is still a good God! So much so, He let His only Son die for us on Calvary. To truly see Calvary is to grasp the charge that Jesus is worthy of all the praise! To embrace the cross is to comprehend whatever suffering we endure is an achievement in fellowship. Yes, life is filled with questions, but they should never deter us from giving God praise. As I began to not just internalize this idea, but declare it deep within me, I wrote words that my fellow laborers in the faith could share.

You Are Worthy

For waking me up early this morning
For starting me on my way
For food on my table
For letting me see another day

For picking me up out of the muck and mire
For taking all my sins away
For peace when in a storm
For keeping me from all hurt and harm

With every fiber in my body
With all of my heart, soul, and mind
I worship You, Heavenly Father
At this appointed time
I'll let nothing get in the way
Of what I've come to say
You are worthy
Of all of the praise that I bring

Only for a While

For his anger lasts only for a moment,
but his favor lasts a lifetime; weeping may remain for a night,
but rejoicing comes in the morning.
Psalm 30:5

This particular Tuesday had been very pleasant. My mother, Ms. Jones, invited me out to lunch. I took her up on the invitation, only to discover, while placing our order at the restaurant, that she wasn't hungry. That was my first test for the day. Thank God I didn't fail it. Ms. Jones really wanted us to spend quality time together. Lunch was an excuse. So, I just sat back and enjoyed the journey. We ran around town like a couple of tourists, stopping here and there with no real agenda to follow.

Evening had set in and our schedule shifted. So did the weather. It began to rain as we headed down the toll-way to Sugar Valley Church for Tuesday Night Bible Study. The rain had become somewhat blinding, yet we kept focused toward our destination. While driving, I decided to call my friend Kim Lun on my cellular phone. My reason for calling was to check up on her and, if necessary, encourage her. She had recently made a major change in her life and I wanted to be guilty of not abandoning her. Furthermore, I was truly concerned about her. As we talked, the rain began pounding on my windshield with great force. Her conversation became much more intense than

I had expected. My attention was then torn between the power of her words and the force of the blinding rain. The script abruptly changed. I called to encourage her, and she began encouraging me. She read to me a scripture that had been shared with her earlier that morning by Beverly Rhodes, a mutual friend. I rejoiced as she read I Peter1:6. We ended our conversation on that high note. Isn't that just like God? He somehow shows up in the midst of inclement weather, whether demonstrated in atmospheric conditions or the spiritual conditions of our lives!

The inspiration for this song text shifts again. After returning home from the remaining of the events of that evening, the wheels in my mind turned with great speed. They settled on a prior lesson taught by Chris Hartwell, pastor at Sugar Valley Church. I reflected on his sentiments concerning James, the servant of God, James 1:2. He made such an impression in my spirit. I, the believer, had been challenged with the truth, according to the Word of God. That truth is, said Pastor Hartwell..."not if, but when, you fall." My complaining ceased at that very moment. Falling is an unavoidable fork along the road of life. God confirms that in His Word. God too confirms in His Word, to the believer, that trials are only for a while. Isn't that just like God? He allows the storm to come, then in time reveals Himself and settles that same storm!

Closure of this text led me toward settling an unresolved storm in my life. The rain no longer blinded my way. The winds of discouragement ceased to affect me. Despite the circumstances ushered in by the tide of life, one thing I do know—change is constant!

Only For A While

The storm is raging all around you
No sign of escape
The lightning's flashing down upon you
So to blind you of your faith
One moment seems like forever
Each step feels like a mile
But in the midst the Father whispers
"It's only for a while"

The thunder's roaring all around you
No sign of relief
The wind is pressing firmly against you
So to hurl you from your feet
Raindrops appear as balls of fire
You feel as helpless as a child
But in the midst the Father whispers
"It's only for a while"

It's only for a while
This thing you're going through
The God of your salvation
Has not forgotten you
He's in control of it all
Not if, but when you fall

Remember, it's only for a while
Even the storm clouds will pass over
The rain in time will cease
Everything has its season
Even days turn into weeks

Holy

In the year that king Uzziah died I saw also the Lord sitting upon a throne, high and lifted up, and his train filled the temple. Above it stood the seraphims; each one had six wings; with twain he covered his face, and with twain he covered his feet, and with twain he did fly. And one cried unto another and said, Holy, holy, holy, is the Lord of hosts; the whole earth is full of his glory. And the posts of the door moved at the voice of him that cried, and the house was filled with smoke.

Isaiah 6:1-8

The ability to worship God with a clear mind is one of the greatest tests for me, the believer. The temptation to repeatedly ask favors of Him, send Him on missions, or register my personal complaints to Him becomes the greater. I am guilty. I have missed golden moments, and forfeited wonderful opportunities to speak of His many attributes. Subsequently I lost by omission, being the recipient of His many benefits. The late Pastor James Henry of Altadena, California said this during one of his prayer seminars...

"When God sees the church praising Him, I can imagine hearing Him saying...Look at my children praising me...let me meet their needs." Just as we reward our children for their obedience to us, so does God. Praise to God is a requirement for me. My praise is an act of obedience to Him.

The period in my life filled with asking God why this, and why that, soon came to end. After six months of questioning God, the Holy Spirit interceded for me. He began to make known my petitions to God, and I was then free to worship God. My mind was then erased of all confusion and distractions, chaos and perplexities. A conscious effort to move in that direction was the forerunner for this process of change. I had to think myself free from all those things that hindered my tongue from speaking praise to God. Prayer became constant. I found myself talking to God regularly, thanking Him, not asking for anything, not making promises to Him, nor complaining, just thanking Him. The result of pertinent private prayer yielded powerful public praise. It was during my private prayer time when so uniquely God revealed Himself to me.

I toiled with this text. I labored with the thought of misrepresenting God and His attributes. To tell the truth, I prayerfully contemplated, carefully placing each word in its proper place. This text is not very long, but very potent. I dared to cloud its contents with only those things that point to the holiness of God. Several attempts preceded the final script. To approach God's Word in song with integrity was my intended pledge. Several days had passed prior to the completion of the 'holy matrimony,' the marriage between the words and music. It was important for each note to compliment each word or syllable. No sound was to overshadow one word in the text. The melodic line, when heard, was to sound like it came from the mind of God Himself. This melody was created by design. It emerged from one whose mind was clear and clean, renewed and transformed. When heard, it should urge others to reverence and respect, bow down and worship the only Holy God.

Furthermore, this text marks the close of a short lived, yet tedious journey, and the start of an exciting walk with the Lord. It is indicative of another chapter ending in my life and a new one beginning. To sing it is like taking a deep breath of fresh air after leaving a smoke filled room. The fragrance of this praise is purposed to God as '*a sweet smelling savor.*' Treat this text with dignity. Sing it with power.

Holy

Holy…Holy
You are Holy
All the earth shall
Bow before Thee
Holy, Holy
You are Holy
All the earth is
Full of Your glory

Consecrated
Pure and Blameless
All the earth shall
Speak Your Splendor
Blessed and Sacred
Clean and Stainless
All the earth shall
Know Your Greatness

You Let Me Know

O give thanks unto the lord, for He is good: for his mercy endureth forever. Let the redeemed of the lord say so, whom he hath redeemed from the hand of the enemy... Oh that men would praise the lord for his goodness, and for his wonderful works to the children of men!

Psalm 107: 1-2, 8

For the Christian songwriter, private moments with God sometimes become public...so public that the whole world has access to those moments. Because we sometimes write from our own personal and private experiences, exposing our hearts to the world, this truth prevails. That is the case with this song. At the beginning of the new millennium, my most intimate moments with God were spent reflecting and thanking. For those simple things He had brought me through, I reflected on them and thanked Him. For those difficult things, I reflected on them and thanked Him.

Hindsight is one of my greatest teachers. However, looking back can be unhealthy. In the case of Lot's wife (Luke 17:32), looking back caused her death. In this scenario, looking back brought me to new hope. Now I possess a greater hope in Jesus Christ, knowing He was with me all along, through all my trials, embarrassments, failures, and temptations. As a matter of fact, it was Jesus who delivered me from all my infirmities. I know surely I did not pull up by my own bootstraps. I am certain that I had no power of my own to handle any of my past situations. In looking back, I saw the hand of God leading me, guiding me, and bringing me through. Every now and then He even carried me, allowing me to feel His love. In looking back and reflecting, I've learned to show gratitude to Him with my total being. In looking back, I know without a doubt that He was always there for me.

He gave this song for me to sing to the world. He brought me to a place in life that was full of joy and expected me to tell of this joy. I wrote this song in February of 2000. It was then He let me look back so that I would know these truths. Once I turned back around, I wrote these words.

You Let Me Know

Through things man could not see
Yet were troubling me
Things that brought me tears
Haunting me for years
Through things I could not share
Consequences too hard to bear
You let me know how much You cared
For me Lord, You were there!

Through nights I laid awake
Clutches I could not shake
Times I tried to give in
Believing I could not win
Through agonizing pain
Indignity and shame
You let me know how much You cared
For me Lord, You were there!

Through trials great and small
Seemingly nothing mattered at all
Issues had me bound
Confusion was all around
In search for peace of mind
I tried You one more time

You let me know how much You cared
For me Lord, You were there!

Hallelujah's in my mouth
Thanksgiving's in my heart
Thoughts of gratitude on my mind
I'll praise you every time
I think of all you've done
The many victories You have won
You let me know how much You cared
For me Lord, You were there

You were there to deliver me
From the hand of the enemy
There to transform my territory
Into a sweet sanctuary
You let me know how much You cared
For me Lord, You were there

Scriptures

A High Cost of Praise - Mark 15:25, 33, 34
Affirmation - 2 Corinthians 1:18-22
All That God Said - Deut. 28:9-13
Anticipation - Revelation - 22:3-4

Before I Tell Them - Luke 10:42
Behind The Curtain - Matthew 12:1-13; Luke 9:28-36

Calvary - Luke 23:33
Creator Of The Valleys - Ezekiel 3:22; Gen. 1:6-7

Eagles' Wings - Isaiah 40:31

For Those Who Love The Lord - Ephesians 6: 23-24
For Tomorrow - Psalm 118:24
From A Distance - Revelations 4:1-11

Go In Peace - 2 Corinthians 1:3-7
Good News - Isaiah 52:7, 53:1
Grace ñ Ephesians 2:4-10

Holy - Isaiah 6:1-8

I Call Him Jesus Christ - Mark 8:27-30
I Am Praying For You - 1 Corinthians 2:11
I Have Fallen In Love With Jesus - Ex. 20:6; Matt.22: 37-38
I'm Still Here - Isaiah 43:1-2
I'm Stronger - 2 Corinthians 4:8-11
In My Dream - Proverbs 13:12
Integrity - Titus 2:6-8
Intercession - Job 42:10-11

Lifting Jesus - John 3:4-5

My Epitaph - Proverbs 15:11
My Time - Psalm 25:1-3
My Way - Luke 15:11-24; Psalm73:1-3

Nevertheless - Luke 5:5
No Walls - Psalm 55:10-14

O Lamb of God - 1 Chronicles 4:9-10
On Eagles Wings - Isaiah 40:27-31
One Thing I Know - John 9:25
Only For A While - Psalm 30:5

Redeemed - Job 33:28
Removal of the Mask - Mark 5:8-9
Resurrection Day - 1 Corinthians 15:12-19
Roof Tearer - Mark 2:4

Save The Boys - 2 Samuel 21:7-14
Say Yes - John 9:35,38; John 11:25-27a
Silent Scream - Lamentations 3:17-26

Speak For Me - Hebrews 7:25

Tell Me - 1 Samuel 9:18-27
The Glad'ning Stream - Psalm 46:4
The Good Shepherd - Psalm 95:7
The Healer - Matthew 4:23-24
The Other Part Of Me - 2 Corinthians 3:16-18
The One Who's Always Looking - Psalm 119:168
The Potter's House - Isaiah 64:8
Through The Storm - Matthew 14:22-23
Turn It Loose - Hebrews 4:16; 7:25

What's In Your Name - Philippians. 2:9-11
When My House Became My Home -
When the Music Stops - Ephesians 5:1-2

You Are Worthy - Revelation 5:11-13
You Let Me Know - Psalm 107: 1-9, 13-15
Your Time is Sure to Come - John 2:1-11

About the Author

For more than a quarter of a century, churches throughout the country have been inspired by the words and music of V. Michael McKay. As a well-respected conductor, clinician, speaker, songwriter, and author, McKay has dedicated his life to a greater level of ministry, with a passion to meet the needs of people in the contemporary Christian community.

McKay is a two-time Dove Award winner and a 2000 inductee into the Gospel Hall of Fame. National artists such as Yolanda Adams, Tramaine Hawkins, and Albertina Walker have recorded his songs. McKay's music is published through Schaff Music Publishing and GIA Publications, Inc. His works are also included in a Southern Baptist hymnal supplement, For the Living of These Days and GIA Publications, Inc.'s groundbreaking African American Heritage Hymnal. His articles related to music ministry have been published in Gospel Industry Today magazine.

V. Michael McKay studied music at both Southern University in Baton Rouge, Louisiana and Texas Southern University. He now resides in Houston, Texas.

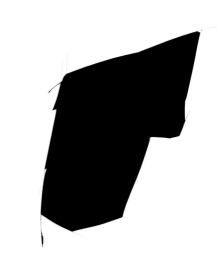

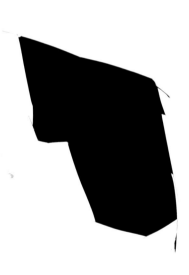